IMAGES
of America

THE HARRIS COMPANY

ON THE COVER: Taken in December 1927 by well-known local photographer Walter Steele, this night shot of the Harris Company on the corner of Third and E Streets in San Bernardino offers a unique view of the new store. (Courtesy of A. K. Smiley Public Library.)

IMAGES
of America

THE HARRIS COMPANY

Aimmee L. Rodriguez,
Richard A. Hanks, and Robin S. Hanks

ARCADIA
PUBLISHING

ISBN 978-0-7385-5901-8

Published by Arcadia Publishing
Charleston, South Carolina

Printed in the United States of America

Library of Congress Catalog Card Number: 2008924117

For all general information contact Arcadia Publishing at:
Telephone 843-853-2070
Fax 843-853-0044
E-mail sales@arcadiapublishing.com
For customer service and orders:
Toll-Free 1-888-313-2665

Visit us on the Internet at www.arcadiapublishing.com

Dedicated to Babette "Bobbie" Meyers, who at age five sent messages through the pneumatic tubes to employees, and to "Hap" and Holly Harris for their unwavering support of this book

Contents

ACKNOWLEDGMENTS

My family moved to the Inland Empire when I was nine. Though the Harris Company by then was a couple decades past its golden era, I could see there was something special about the Harris Company building. In 1999, I wrote a paper on the Harris Company for a graduate history class that eventually became my master's thesis. I wish to thank my mentors whose advice through the years has guided my steps in my passion for this old department store: Colleen O'Connor, Iris Engstrand, Milford Wayne Donaldson, James Sandos, and Larry Burgess. I would also like to thank the following individuals for their support and assistance on this project: Steven Shaw, Richard Thompson, Nathan Gonzales, John Adams, Milly Lugo, Chris Jepsen, William J. Butler, Lily Fontamillas Layon, Russ Keller, Paul Garrety, Sue Payne, Chris Shovey, Jim Petrucci, Linda Puetz, Dave Rutherfurd, Donna McCune, Timothy Sumerlee, Brian Concannon, and Jorge Pont. Special thanks also goes to Harris family members Harriet, Geoff, and Barbara Engel, Hap and Holly Harris, and Bobbie Meyers. Harriet and Hap's generous donation of photographs, scrapbooks, and ephemera made this book possible. Finally, to my coauthors Richard and Robin Hanks, thank you for your work and talent that make this an Inland Empire book, and for all the soup and laughs that made this enjoyable.

—Aimmee Rodriguez

The bulk of our thanks goes to Dr. Jacqueline Davison Lee, who loaned us her mother's collection of photographs, letters, and newspaper articles, and to Joan H. Hall, who loaned us her personal collection of Harris materials and research. These collections were invaluable in writing captions for the Early Beginnings, Redlands, and Riverside chapters. We would also like to thank the following people for their help: Pauline Tingey, Burna Button, Jana McIver, and Judi Mosby. Finally, we would like to thank our coauthor Aimmee Rodriguez for giving us the opportunity to work with her on this project and to add a little of our own personal history with the Harris Company.

—Richard and Robin Hanks

All images appearing in this book were graciously provided by the San Bernardino Historical and Pioneer Society, the California Room in the Norman F. Feldheym Central Library, the Rialto Historical Society, and the Heritage Room of A. K. Smiley Public Library unless otherwise noted.

FOREWORD

For almost a century, the store my grandfather and great uncles founded was a pillar of the San Bernardino community. As they wrote in the Harris Company mission statement, "Be conscious of civic responsibilities—share time and resources for community advancement." As a third-generation owner and operator of the Harris' chain of stores—anchored in the big San Bernardino location and reaching as far north as Bakersfield and west to Riverside—I used this credo in all my dealings with our customers. Service to our neighbors was part of the original business model.

Each succeeding generation of Harris men was expected to join in the family business. When I took up the helm, I had more than 60 years of the Harris reputation behind me. Early on, our stores were often the centers of commerce in the cities in which they were built. In the days before large super-stores that are the same from town to town, my family's stores were places people wanted to go, and were a unique experience in shopping. We offered value; an attractive, safe environment; and a sense that we were not merely a business but a real member of the community.

I remember fondly the wonderful atmosphere of our flagship store in San Bernardino. On any given day, you could shop for furniture on the third floor, have lunch on the mezzanine, or during Uncle Leslie's era for some special occasion, take a pony ride on the roof. Although our stores have changed hands and the beautiful San Bernardino location is now empty, the Harris Company lives on in the communities we helped to build and in the memories we share. Think of the thousands of people who got their first pair of shoes at one of my family's stores or bought a wedding dress or an anniversary gift. I am glad I had the opportunity to share my family's legacy with them.

—Harold C. "Hap" Harris

SHOPPING AT THE HARRIS COMPANY. From the 1930s through the 1960s, a trip to the Harris Company was more than shopping—it was an event. People often dressed in their best—shorts or capri pants were too casual—and traveled to San Bernardino from as far away as the High Desert or the local mountains. They came to experience the relaxed and cool environment that was the Harris Company. Local teenagers commonly rode a bus to the store and lunched at Woolworth's, Annabelle's, the Chinese Gardens, or Harris' Café Madrid. They finished their day with a movie at the Ritz, Crest, or California Theaters. One of Southern California's most prominent merchandising institutions started as the family-owned Harris' in San Bernardino, California. As its reputation and success grew, it became known as the Harris Company, housed in a 200,000-square-foot department store with distinctive architectural details that matched its reputation for quality and service. In its last decades, the store was known simply as "Harris' Co.," yet through all the changes, Harris customers remained loyal to the end.

INTRODUCTION

The story of the Harris Company is a truly American one. It was a family business, founded by three immigrant brothers from Germany. They were descendants of the Herschkowitz family, which had a long history of mercantilism in Germany. In 1885, the eldest of the three, Philip Harris, then only 17, found work with relatives in the mercantile business in Santa Ana. There he learned his trade and opened his own business in the 1890s. His brother Herman Harris arrived in 1887 at the age of 16 with only $2.40 in his pocket. Hard work and savings enabled him to reach Southern California, and he found work in San Bernardino and, finally, Santa Ana in 1893, where he remained for 11 years.

In 1905, Herman returned to San Bernardino, where he joined with his brother Philip in a dry-goods operation with a total of three employees. The business prospered, and soon another brother, Arthur, joined the venture, and the Harris Company was born.

In 1908, the company expanded with the opening of a store in nearby Redlands, replacing the Merriman Randall dry-goods store on Orange Street. Philip moved his family to Redlands and managed that store until his death in 1939. Business was brisk enough to trade locations with the Redlands Hardware Company in 1915. Two years later, the Redlands store was expanded into the adjoining Smith Brothers Oriental Gift Store. Disaster struck the Redlands store in 1925 when fire leveled the building. In the spirit that made Harris' great, business was suspended for only one day. A new location was secured, decorated by students from the University of Redlands, and friends and employees worked around the clock stocking the temporary location with inventory for the public. People remembered how Herman Harris took charge even before the last flames had died out.

By 1927, the partnership of the three brothers had grown into a corporation worth $1 million. The flagship store in San Bernardino at the corner of Third and E Streets was the cornerstone of the city's business district. Local architect Howard E. Jones built the structure in a Spanish Renaissance style. With its alternating stonework and grillwork detail, and the Harris family coat-of-arms molded within the stonework's façade, the three-story building was reminiscent of the finest stores in Europe.

For patrons of the store, the Harris Company became synonymous with quality and personalized service. For their employees and the communities they served, Harris' meant loyalty and commitment. The company weathered the Great Depression of the 1930s by trimming salaries but not the roster of workers. Herman Harris was even credited with stopping a run on a local bank. By World War II, a second generation of Harris brothers was at the helm of the prospering corporation and brought innovative ideas to faithful shoppers. Animated Christmas window displays, Santa in Toyland, Men's Night, and fashion shows excited and entertained all those who eagerly shopped at one of their stores. They became the style center of San Bernardino with a tea room, gown shop, Café Madrid, beauty parlor and barber shop, book department, and lending library. They were the first to introduce electric signs, elevators, and escalators to the public.

Their continued success led to the opening of a Riverside store in 1957 as the anchor for the city's first mall, the Riverside Plaza. The Riverside Harris Company brought with it all the amenities that engaged people at the other locations. People fondly remember visiting Harris' for their first experience with Santa, or taking tea with girlfriends on a warm afternoon, or thrilling to the sight of a Harris' fashion show. Some recall the excitement of buying their first prom dress at a Harris store or even meeting a future husband who caught their eye in front of a display window. Harris' was more than a department store—it was a place of memories.

The Harris Company's flagship store in San Bernardino closed in 1999 when the chain merged with the Gottschalks department stores. It was a sad farewell for thousands of former patrons throughout the Inland Empire. Before strip malls and cookie-cutter outlets, the Harris Company represented stores personalized to their customers' tastes, where you shopped with people you knew and trusted. It was a slower, quieter time when people took the time to know each other. For the many who remember a Harris Company experience, a nostalgic—if wistful—smile takes them back to a memory of a day that somehow seemed better.

One

The Harris Family and Early Beginnings

Family Reunion, 1909. The Harris family had a reunion at the home of William and Regina Falkenstein in Anaheim, California. The gathering was to celebrate the visit of Dr. Lesser Herschkowitz from San Francisco. Johanna (seated, center) was Morris' second wife. She had seven children with him but raised the entire clan as if they were her own. Pictured here from left to right are (first row) Morrey Anker, Alvin Asher, Melville Harris, Harold Harris, and Stanley Falkenstein; (second row) William Falkenstein, Regina Harris Falkenstein, Leah Steinart Harris, Gertrude Asher, Johanna Harris, Eda Harris Asher, Rose Harris Anker, and Herman Harris; (third row) Arthur Harris, Philip Harris, Leslie Harris, Isadore Asher, Selmar Anker, Dr. Lesser Herschkowitz, and Rudolph Anker.

PATRIARCH OF THE HARRIS FAMILY. Morris Herschkowitz was a merchant and owner of business properties in West Prussia. He came to America in 1848 to seek freedom, settling first in Georgia and later in Kentucky. In 1853, he returned to Germany to visit his parents, married, and had four children, Emma, Rose, Zara, and Lesser, before his wife died of childbirth complications. He eventually remarried and had seven more children: Eda, Philip, Herman, Leo, Hulda, Regina, and Arthur. As Morris and, later, his sons, came to America, Morris' brother, Leopold Harris, of Harris & Frank in Los Angeles, advised them to drop the family name Herschkowitz for Harris.

FIVE HARRIS BROTHERS, C. 1909. Pictured here from left to right are Philip, Leo, Arthur, Lesser, and Herman. Philip, Herman, and Arthur were the brothers that started the Harris Company. Their younger brother Leo ran a country store in Lancaster in 1912. His interest, however, was more in line with land management. He owned considerable acreage in alfalfa and even had interest in a gold mine. Their older brother Lesser obtained his medical degree under the name Herschkowitz from the School of Medicine at the University of Berlin. Thus, he was the only one of the Harris children to retain the family name. He practiced in Los Angeles then moved to San Francisco in 1896. He was a noted physician and served on the California State Board of Medical Examiners.

PHILIP HARRIS, C. 1895. When Philip first arrived in 1885, he worked for his brother-in-law Rudolph Anker, a dry-goods merchant in San Bernardino, California. He was not too impressed with the dusty little town and left to work for another brother-in-law, Simon Goldsmith, a dry-goods and shoe merchant, in Santa Ana. In 1893, Philip married Anna Hirschfield and proceeded to start his family. They had three sons: Leslie, Harold, and Melville. After a couple ventures with his brother Herman, he left to work as a salesman for his uncle Leopold of Harris & Frank in Los Angeles. In April 1905, Philip returned to San Bernardino to open Harris' with his brother Herman. Seven months later, his wife passed away. With hard work and the help of his sisters to watch over Melville, Harris' was a success. Two years later, Philip married Leah Steinart. Early employees remember Philip greeting the salesladies with a cheery, "Good morning, merry sunshine." When Philip left the San Bernardino store in 1909 to manage the new Harris store in Redlands, the employees sorely missed him.

First location in San Bernardino, California, 1905. Harris' first location was on the bottom floor of the Armory Building at 462 Third Street between D and E Streets. They had a mere 25 feet of store frontage and an upstairs neighbor called Company "K," who were lucky enough to have a balcony on which to watch parades. The store's opening was announced in the local newspaper: "On Wednesday, April 19, we will formally open our doors to the public of San Bernardino and vicinity. . . . A cordial invitation to visit our store is extended to all. We are strangers among you, but have come to stay and we want to get acquainted. . . . We have come here prepared in every way to do a large Dry Goods business. If courteous treatment, low prices, good goods and honest methods are appreciated here then we will certainly have no difficulty in gaining your trade. We mean every word we say and say just what we mean. . . . try us. Harris' has it for less."

HERMAN HARRIS, C. 1895. Herman came to America in 1887, two years after his brother Philip. He followed in his brother's footsteps, working first for brother-in-law Rudolph Anker, then brother-in-law Simon Goldsmith. In 1893, Simon rented the building he owned to Philip on 116 West Fourth Street, and the brothers opened their own dry-goods business called the White House. Two years later, when Philip and his family left for Los Angeles, Herman kept the shop and changed the name to H. Harris Company. In April 1905, Rudolph convinced Herman to return to San Bernardino. He closed out his Santa Ana store and brought $4,700 worth of stock with him. With optimism and the firm belief in the growth of San Bernardino, Herman wrote the advertisements, oversaw office work, and waited on customers when the clerks were busy. An early employee recalled that Herman was a walking business barometer. When things were bright and sunny, he whistled "The Spring Maid." When merchandise moved slowly, he whistled "Miserere" from *Il Trovatore*. He remained a bachelor, his family citing the business as the love of his life.

INTERIOR OF HARRIS' FIRST LOCATION, 1905. Herman and Philip began with a staff of three to help them in their new business. Flossie Annable was hired to work in the office, Millie Hage was the fitter, and Mintce Conway was the saleslady. After a short time, Flossie got married, and Rosa Kramer was hired to take her place.

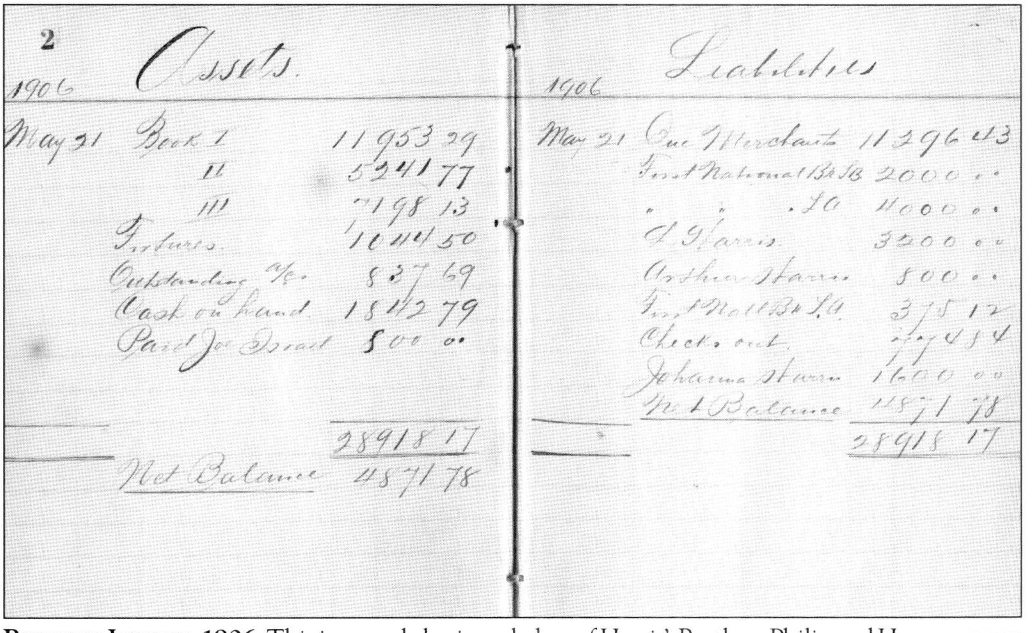

1906	Assets.		1906	Liabilities	
May 21	Book I	11953 29	May 21	Due Merchants	11296 43
	II	5241 77		First National Bk SB	2000 00
	III	7198 13		" " LA	4000 00
	Fixtures	1044 50		A. Harris	3200 00
	Outstanding a/c	837 69		Arthur Harris	800 00
	Cash on hand	1842 79		First Natl Bk LA	375 12
	Paid Jos. Israel	500 00		Checks out	774 84
				Johanna Harris	1600 00
				Net Balance	4871 78
		28918 17			28918 17
	Net Balance	4871 78			

BUSINESS LEDGER, 1906. This is an early business ledger of Harris'. Brothers Philip and Herman came to San Bernardino in 1905 with $4,700 worth of stock from the dry-goods store Herman previously owned in Santa Ana. Just one year and one month later, they achieved a balance of $4,871.78.

ARTHUR HARRIS, C. 1900. Arthur arrived in 1893. With his brothers established in Santa Ana, he first worked for Herman, then for his brothers-in-law Isadore Asher and William Falkenstein in Anaheim, California. When Arthur joined his brothers in San Bernardino in 1906, he brought $2,500 with him, which aided in the move to Harris' second location, the Jospeh Israel store. Arthur used to drive a horse-and-buggy to work and would often give the salesladies a lift. He married Hertha Horowitz in 1916, and they had two daughters: Barbara and Norma. When the Harris Company moved to its third location in 1927, Arthur was the most visible of the brothers. He greeted customers on the main floor and knew many by name.

SECOND LOCATION IN SAN BERNARDINO, CALIFORNIA, 1906. Harris' moved across the street in 1906 to the Joseph Israel store. A third brother, Arthur, joined them, bringing $2,500, which allowed them to hire a window trimmer and a dozen employees. Harris' window displays gave them the distinction of being known as the style center of the city.

SECOND FLOOR EXPANSION, 1907. One year after the move, Harris' outgrew its first floor space. Frames, feathers, and flowers were on the notions tables, and hats were scattered on any available space throughout the store. Harris' took over the second floor to house their ready-to-wear and millinery departments. By 1908, Harris' installed the first elevator in San Bernardino, attracting much attention; it was the first one seen by many.

EARLY WINDOW DISPLAY, 1913. Dubbed the Marshall Field's of San Bernardino, the Harris Company was awarded a $100 prize for its display windows. A publication stated that Harris' display windows indicated the artistic and cosmopolitan character of the valley's residents. The Harris Company was seen as both progressive and successful in displaying the latest fashionable styles and would not be surpassed by the finest of stores on the East Coast.

EXPANSIONS FOR HARRIS', C. 1917. By 1915, Harris' was bursting at the seams, allowing for the purchase of Pritchard's next door, with its huge electric sign—the first in the city—and its luxurious restrooms that were advertised near and far. One wall was taken out and made into an archway to connect the two stores. Eventually, Harris' also bought out their brother-in-law Rudolph Anker's clothing store (left).

World War I Parade, 1918. A World War I parade on Third Street shows Harris' first location at the Armory Building (third from left) and second location across the street (balcony outcropping). Harris' inherited the first electrical sign in the city, which is faintly visible on the roof beyond the first electrical pole on the right.

Harris' Bargain Annex, 1919. The Harris' Bargain Annex was located on the southeast corner of Third and D Streets. Management devised a way to liquidate their stock of odds and ends, and to prune out old or incomplete clothing lines by offering them at hugely reduced prices. They hoped to appeal to the thrifty shopper. The Bargain Annex closed in 1922 and was replaced by Market Spot in 1923.

HARRIS' REMOVAL SALE, 1927. It was fortunate that the move to the new store was close to year's end. Certain stock would not be brought to the new store and, therefore, was greatly reduced. The store promoted the savings that could be had for the upcoming winter season and said it would be years, if ever, before the public would see such genuine bargains again.

MOVING IN, 1927. Early employees recalled packing merchandise into canvas carts and rolling them through the streets. Showcases were put on dollies and moved during the night. Everyone was glad to say good-bye to smoky oil stoves and looked forward to the modern facility. Employees were excited and pleased to arrange stock in the beautiful new store. In this photograph, employees are moving the switchboard onto the loading dock.

MELVILLE AND LESLIE HARRIS, 1930. This photograph was taken on September 23, 1930, by Arthur Brayton, with an inscription on the back that reads, "Hope to use this in Journal soon." It shows 28-year-old Melville (left) and 36-year-old Leslie in front of the Harris Company display windows on E Street. Known among the employees as "Mr. Melville" and "Mr. Leslie," they were the living evidence of the hope their father and grandfather brought with them to America—success can be had with opportunity and hard work. Though the Great Depression was still fresh, optimism and pride remained on the faces of these young entrepreneurs. Reflected in the window behind them is the Stewart Hotel.

PHILIP HARRIS HOME, REDLANDS, CALIFORNIA, 1927. These exterior and interior photographs show the home of Philip Harris, located at 228 Grandview Drive in Redlands, California. Philip moved to Redlands in 1909 to take over the management of the new Redlands store and remained there until his death in 1939, when he was succeeded by his son Harold.

HAROLD HARRIS HOME, REDLANDS, CALIFORNIA, 1927. The honeymoon home of Harold C. Harris Sr. was located at 123 Garden Hill Drive in Redlands, California. When Harold graduated from high school in 1915, he began working full time as his father's assistant in yardage at the Redlands store. In 1925, he became general buyer and floor manager, and in 1939, following his father's death, he became manager of the Redlands store.

SECOND GENERATION OF HARRIS BROTHERS, C. 1965. Philip's sons (pictured here from left to right) Melville, Leslie, and Harold embraced the family legacy of community involvement and civic leadership. Their combined accomplishments were extensive. From the local Boy Scouts to war bond drives of World War II; from family services to the Red Cross, they never hesitated to give back to the public they served. Under their business acumen, the Harris Company built traditions such as Men's Night, Santa at Harris' Toyland, Girl of the Week, and knitting classes. Their stores provided not just merchandise but memories.

PLAQUE HONORING THE FOUNDING BROTHERS, 1955. Philip, Herman, and Arthur launched a business in 1905 that became a distinctive merchandising institution in Southern California. They proved the old 14th-century proverb that "great oaks from little acorns grow." Their philosophy to "build for tomorrow with vision and courage without forgetting the needs of today" gave them the opportunity to live what they preached. The organizations they helped to found, assisted, or chaired are numerous. They served as directors for local chambers of commerce and for the National Orange Show, and they generously supported the surrounding universities, local hospitals, and local musical associations. Pictured here is an employee gift to the second generation of the Harris family at the 50th anniversary celebration.

Family Dinner Party. After Philip passed away, his wife, Leah, lived at the Arrowhead Springs Hotel for a time. She was known as the belle of the place. Pictured here is Leah, hosting the engagement dinner for Harriet and William Engel. Clockwise from bottom left are Harold, Frances, Babette, Hertha, Leslie, Jeannette, Arthur, Leah, William, Harriet, Melville, Marcelle, Hap, and Andree Lehman (Marcelle's mother).

Leslie Harris, President and General Manager of the Harris Company. Like his father and uncles, Leslie learned the business the hard way. He recalled how on his way to school he had to open up shop, sweep out the store, and, in winter, start the wood fires. He peddled advertising bills for 20¢ for 100 until he lost the seat of his pants to a dog bite.

Partial Harris Family Tree. Pictured are four generations of Harris family members who worked at the Harris Company.

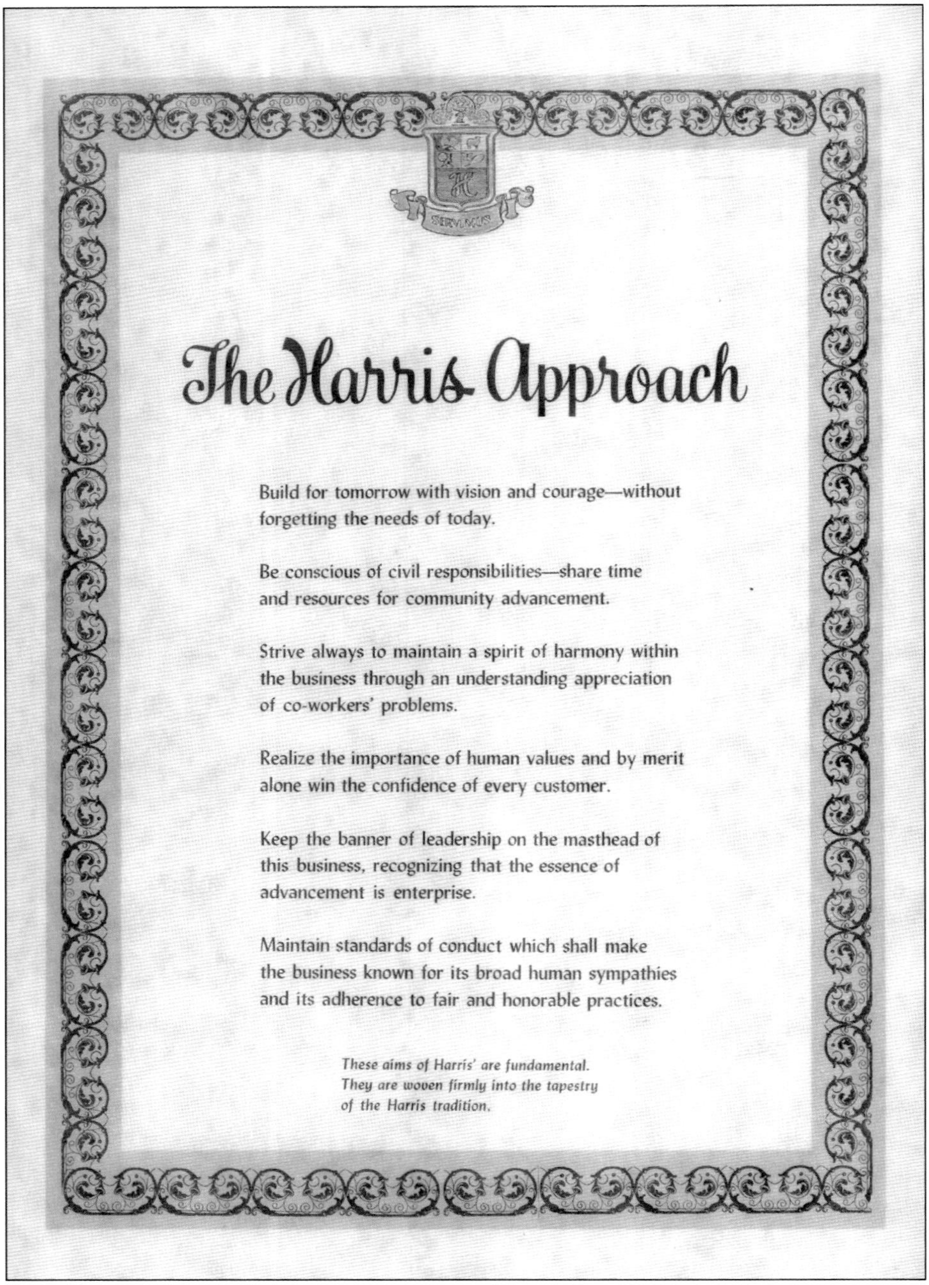

The Harris Approach

Build for tomorrow with vision and courage—without forgetting the needs of today.

Be conscious of civil responsibilities—share time and resources for community advancement.

Strive always to maintain a spirit of harmony within the business through an understanding appreciation of co-workers' problems.

Realize the importance of human values and by merit alone win the confidence of every customer.

Keep the banner of leadership on the masthead of this business, recognizing that the essence of advancement is enterprise.

Maintain standards of conduct which shall make the business known for its broad human sympathies and its adherence to fair and honorable practices.

These aims of Harris' are fundamental. They are woven firmly into the tapestry of the Harris tradition.

THE HARRIS APPROACH. Today "The Harris Approach" would be known as a company's mission statement. The Harris Company, however, was not a typical business. While profit is important in any business, it was not the company's only bottom line. In the early days, the Harris Company promoted development of the cities in which it did business. The company was active in its civic responsibilities, earning respect in the communities. As a sole entity, the Harris Company took time to ensure it had strong relationships with its employees. As a result, the employees took pains to see that customers were properly attended. The Harris Company was committed to service, integrity, quality, and value, and it was proud to be known as "The Store for all the People."

Two

The Harris Company in San Bernardino

The Harris Company Department Store, 1927. The building housed a basement, first floor, mezzanine level, second floor, third floor, and roof garden. It was constructed as a fireproof structure that would include all the modern amenities of the time. The southeast corner of the building had a staircase of colorful tiles, which led to their restaurant, Café Madrid. The building's doors were made of hammered copper. The structure revealed a face to match the Harris Company's reputation of quality and service. The building in San Bernardino was significant. The Harris Company was the first major department store to set up shop in the Inland Empire, thereby giving the region prominence. The local newspaper stated the importance when it reported, "towns do not have department stores. The Inland Empire has arrived." The Harris Company is pictured here less than a month before the official opening.

CONSTRUCTION OF THE HARRIS COMPANY, 1927. In 1919, the management of the Harris Company began to acquire property on the corner of Third and E Streets. Many smaller buildings, such as the San Bernardino Brewery, later known as the Andreson Brewery, were on this site, and it took time to acquire the needed land. Demolition and excavation did not commence until 1927. This photograph shows the progress of construction two months and 21 days before the official opening.

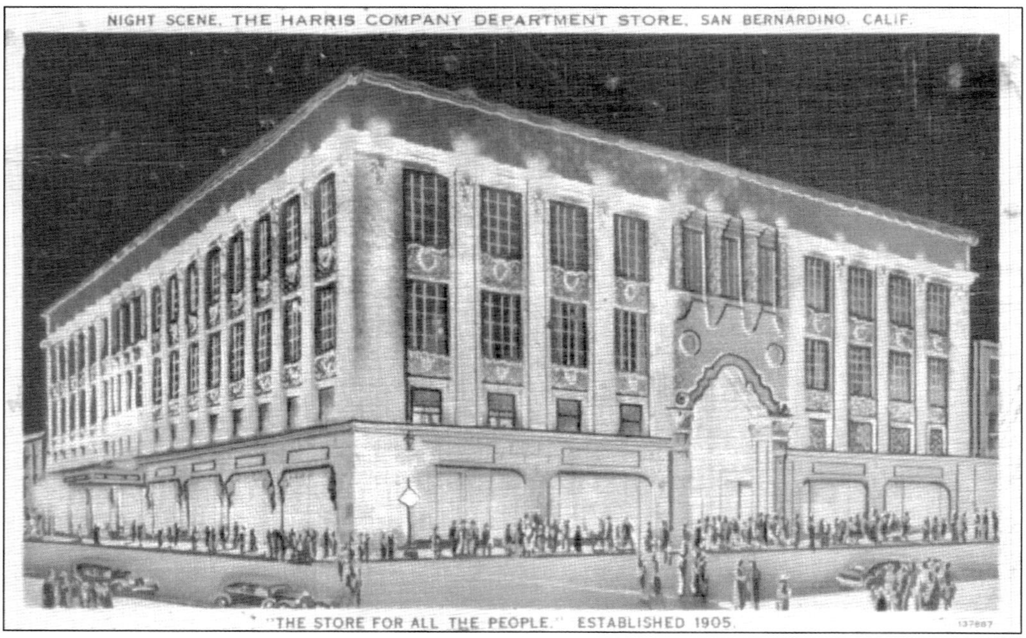

OPENING DAY, NOVEMBER 7, 1927. The Harris Company department store opened on the corner of Third and E Streets in November 1927. Local architect Howard E. Jones built the structure in the Spanish Renaissance style. Molded within the stonework's façade was the Harris coat-of-arms, similar to the style used in businesses in Europe. Many considered the store to be the cornerstone of San Bernardino's business district.

DEDICATION

The building is finished, the task is done,
Our heart-dream of years has come true!
It stands as a monument fairly won—
A monument builded by YOU.

Your loyalty ever encouraged our growth,
Your friendships are true to the core
And helpful to harvest the seeds we sowed;
Your confidence builded this store!

The foundation stones that carry the weight
Of this structure of concrete and steel
Are deeply embedded in faith in God—
This is His benediction, we feel.

The mighty frame as it solidly stands
Embracing its place in the mart,
Embraces, also, the good will of men;
Good will, most prized in each heart.

The lintels and beams their significance lend:
As symbols they plainly express
The binding together, throughout the years,
Of friendships that make for success.

The eyes of the store are its windows and light,
As are the eyes to the soul;
We'll keep them clear by day and by night
As forward we march to our goal.

The men and women, CO-workers for years,
Who strived for our aims and our ends,
Who shared our struggles and hopes and fears,
We name them our loyal friends.

And, so, to the Giver of all good gifts
Our thanks for this building we tend;
Inspire our actions in honor, and truth,
And righteousness, God, to the end!

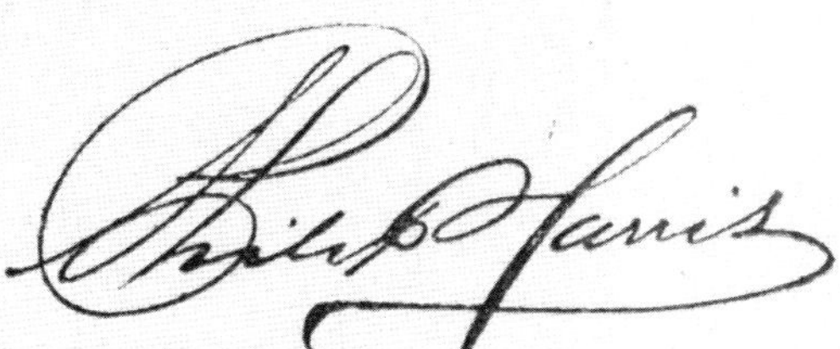

DEDICATION OF THE HARRIS COMPANY, 1927. At the 50th anniversary celebration, Melville Harris said, "in April 1905 [the founders] planted that small acorn, nurtured and watched over it, sheltered it against many a storm, and lived to see it grow to maturity and bear fruit." The Harris Company building exemplified the founders' faith in the future growth of San Bernardino. The poem (above), written by Philip Harris, was printed in the local newspaper the day before the store officially opened. He remembered the early days of "sweeping out the [little] store in the morning, to unpacking wooden cases of calico, as well as covering up the goods at night with unbleached muslin," and eloquently expressed his humble gratitude to the community that helped to make the family-owned company great.

HARRIS COMPANY MAIN ENTRANCE, 1927. The main entrance archway of the Harris Company department store was fitted with Italian marble and rose 29 feet. The interior lobby ceiling was an impressive 32 feet high and displayed colors such as soft reds, golds, and blues reminiscent of Tuscany, Italy. This photograph was taken by Walter Steele, a local photographer, for an article in the local newspaper announcing the Harris Company's official opening on the following day.

VIEW OF THE MAIN FLOOR, C. 1927. This postcard view states that the Harris Company is housed in a modern department store building. It has a café, fountain, luncheonette, beauty salon, and basement beauty shop, free auto parking, rest rooms, lounge, roof garden, public telephones, information desk, sub-express office, free portal checking, lending library, shoe repair, gift wrapping, and mailing service. The Harris Company also offered free delivery to anywhere in the Inland Empire.

HARRIS COMPANY BASEBALL TEAM, C. 1927. The demise of the Harris Company baseball team occurred after one member broke his ankle during a game and began to draw workman's compensation. The Harris Company was the first institution in the valley to offer group life, health, and accident insurance, and it later offered medical and hospital insurance. Baseball games, however, were thought better left to employees' personal time.

GOWN SHOP, 1940. The gown shop was located on the northeast corner of the second floor. Sandra Wilson was the bridal secretary and fashion coordinator in the late 1940s. She assisted San Bernardino valley brides in choosing outfits for their wedding parties, filled their hope chests, and drew up budgets for their linen trousseaus. (Courtesy of the San Bernardino County Museum.)

MEN'S DEPARTMENT. Men's Night was a program initiated in the late 1940s. On certain nights, only men were allowed into the store. Clerks, mostly older women, would assist the men in shopping for Christmas gifts for their wives, girlfriends, or children. This service was another feature that lent distinction to the Harris Company.

YARDAGE DEPARTMENT. The yardage deparment was located on the mezzanine level. One customer recalled spending time sitting on the tall stools. She and her mother would look through big pattern books for all the sewing they planned to do. Tables filled with bolts of fabric gave them a large variety to choose from. On occasion, one of the salesladies even taught girls to embroider between helping customers.

NOTIONS DEPARTMENT. The notions department carried accessories such as buttons, zippers, beads, ribbon, and trim. Before and after ready-to-wear clothing was available, sewing was both utilitarian and artful. Many women sewed clothes for themselves and their family. This view of the notions department on the third floor shows the Harris Company windows from the inside.

ALTERNATE VIEW OF MAIN FLOOR, C. 1927. Inland Empire valley residents now had a grand department store that stood out as the most fashionable and classy in the region. The Harris Company was likened to Bullock's in Los Angeles and Marshall Fields in Chicago. One early employee put it best when she said, "It was a palace." The main floor is seen here from the mezzanine.

ONE YEAR AFTER COMPLETION, 1928. One year after completion, the Harris Company stood proud with 42 departments. To meet strong demand, features were added such as the creative women's department, the piano studio, and a storytelling hour for children. With the telegraph, modern at the time, and air-mail service, the Harris Company connected local valley shoppers to New York, the center of the fashion world.

ROOF GARDEN, 1930. The Harris Company had a roof garden that, in the early days, was rented to local organizations for parties. During Leslie Harris' era, pony rides were even given on the roof. An early Harris Company employee handbook boldly invited them to take advantage of the fresh air. A former employee remembered quite a few staff parties held on the roof. Everyone would dress up and go dancing, and sometimes brothers Leslie and Melville Harris would join in too.

THE HARRIS COMPANY DURING THE DEPRESSION, C. 1930. In 1927, some San Bernardino banks thought it a gamble for the Harris brothers to build a modern, $500,000 department store in a town of roughly 20,000 people. That risk was realized two years later when the panic of the Great Depression began closing banks across the country. When the banks that backed the Harris Company were threatened, Herman and his nephew Leslie devised a plan to save at least one of the banks. Gathering money from store operations, regular deposits were made by the controller, Joe Hawkins, into Harris accounts. Herman stood atop a chair and shouted to nervous patrons, "We are making deposits all through the day for the Harris Company." This prompted other leading citizens to join in, expressing confidence in the bank. A hastily painted sign reading "New Accounts Accepted Here" was displayed, and as many Harris employees as possible were dispatched to the bank to open small accounts. News of Herman's actions circulated around town. R. D. McCook, cofounder of the bank, credited Herman with stopping the panic and saving the bank.

HARRIS' MONTHLY STORE NEWS, 1934. Started in 1919 and later known as the *Harris Booster News*, the company produced an in-house newsletter on company events, employee marriages, illnesses, births, deaths, travel, and company improvement. The original officers came up with a cheer that emphasized the Harris Company team spirit: "Yes, we're the Booster Club of Harris Store, We're all for one, and one for all, We'll work together for the Harris store, in summer, spring, and fall, We'll pull together every single day, We'll boost each other all along the way, and with a smile upon our lips we'll say, 'The Booster Club, Hip-hip hooray!" Pulling together had wider meaning than just inside Harris stores as the blue eagle logo on the *Booster News* indicates. The logo represented the National Recovery Act, passed by the Roosevelt administration during the darkest days of the Depression. Codes incorporated in the act regulated wages and prices, and sought to eliminate unfair business practices. Stores like Harris', which adopted the codes, proudly displayed the logo and its motto, "We do our part."

CORNER OF THIRD AND E STREETS, 1940S. Cruising the streets of downtown San Bernardino was a regular pastime even during the war. One customer remembered hanging out with girlfriends in front of the second set of the Harris Company's display windows south of Third Street. A sailor on leave passed by in a car with another fellow and happened to catch her eye. They went on a date the next night, and he asked her to marry him.

THE HARRIS COMPANY SUPPORTS THE TROOPS, 1943. The Harris family took its role as business leaders in the community seriously. On July 7, 1943, the Harris Company placed an advertisement in the local newspaper to "Knit Something for the Boys." The next month, management invited the U.S. Marine Corps to establish an information booth on the store's main floor.

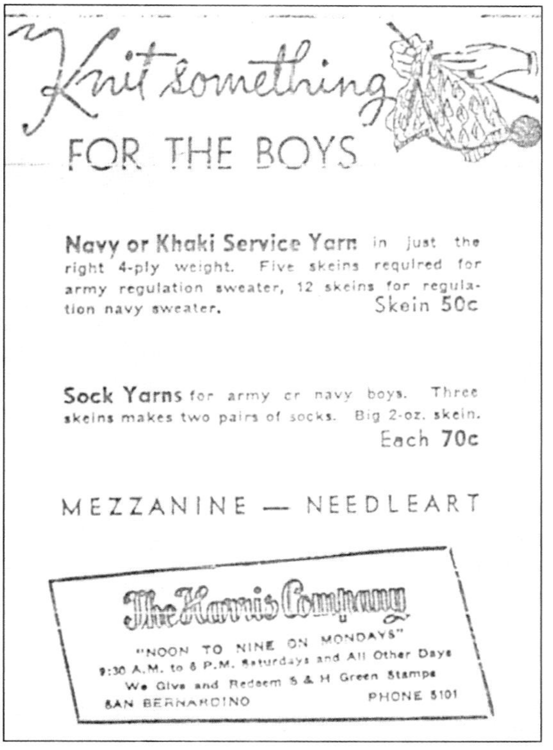

THE HARRIS COMPANY AND THE UNITED NATIONS, 1945. On April 25, 1945, the Harris Company took out a three-quarter-page advertisement in the local newspaper, sending hopeful prayers for the convening of the new United Nations. The Harris brothers were influenced by their grandfather, who fled his native Germany for the freedom America offered. Their unabashed patriotism showed great faith in God, country, and their fellow man.

LIVE BROADCAST, 1940S. Live promotional broadcasts were commonplace during the early years of radio. Here a Harris Company bridal event was aired live over historic San Bernardino station KFXM, originally housed in the California Hotel. Participants are Arthur Harris (left), an unidentified spokeswoman, and Leslie Harris. The call letters KFXM were first used in 1929, and the station continued until 1988. A young Tennessean, Ernie Ford, was a disc jockey in 1946.

INAUGURATION OF THE MOTORSTAIRS, 1947. The Harris Company was the first building in the Inland Empire to have a motorstair, or escalator, as it is known today. Arthur Harris noted that the installation was the culmination of 42 years of effort, faith, and confidence in the future of San Bernardino. Customers felt appreciation that the Harris Company gave San Bernardino everything the big cities had.

MOTORSTAIR CELEBRATION, 1947. After the inauguration ceremony, one boy was denied his turn since he wore no shoes. His brother, however, rode to the top and, after coming back down, loaned his shoes to his sibling so he could have a turn too. For the next three days, parents knew exactly where to find their children when they shopped. The motorstair created quite a stir, since the closest alternative was an hour away in Los Angeles.

BOOK DEPARTMENT AND LENDING LIBRARY, 1947. The Harris Company community projects included sponsoring book-report contests. Winners received $10 to spend on any book they wanted. A customer fondly recalled getting lost in Nancy Drew mysteries while her mother paid a bill at the credit department. Another remembered the lending library was so popular because its books were a bit racier than those at the local library.

RECORD DEPARTMENT, 1947. Personal appearances by famous personalities—such as the Toni Twins—were not uncommon at the Harris Company. Invitations to home economists, actors, artists, and authors had been extended as early as 1933. Pictured here (center) is Tex Williams, one of Capitol Record's recording artists from the late 1940s, meeting Harris customers and signing records.

Harris Company Cashiers, 1947. Before cash registers existed at each department counter, money was sent through pneumatic tubes to a centralized cashier. Change would be made, sent back through the tubes, and the transaction would be completed. The Harris Company cashiers were on the mezzanine level. Pictured here from left to right are Eloise Mailhoit, Laura Whitfield, and assistant cashier Opal Harrison.

The "Ding-Ding" Sound, 1947. The pneumatic tube system, like arteries of communication, ran from every cashier to every department throughout the entire store. After installation of the motorstairs, however, many shoppers became aware of a "ding-ding" sound in the store. Random in occurrence and frequency, people wondered if it was coming from the elevators, escalators, or pneumatic tubes (seen here above the escalator). The mysterious "ding-ding" was actually the Harris Company paging system.

HARRIS COMPANY ANIMATED CHRISTMAS DISPLAY WINDOWS. An annual Christmas tradition for many Inland Empire residents was to stop and see the Harris Company display windows on E Street. Whether filled with an animated Santa and elves or other Christmas scenes, the windows elicited collective "oohs" and "ahhs" from the crowd of onlookers. Perfume was sprayed from the main entrance, and a huge Christmas tree dominated the middle of the first floor under the clock.

HARRIS' TOYLAND ADVERTISEMENT, 1936. During the holiday season, the Harris Company toy department would be transformed into a winter wonderland. One customer remembered a Lionel train running through a miniature village when he was a boy. This advertisement announces Santa's arrival from the North Pole and advises customers to tune into KFXM from 5:30 to 6:00 p.m. to listen to *The Christmas Tree*.

THE HARRIS COMPANY SANTA, c. 1930. Numerous children met their first Santa Claus at Harris' Toyland. For many years, the Harris Company had the only Santa in the region. Toyland was originally in the basement (as pictured above). Ted Brotherton was the Harris Company Santa in 1928. Pictured below are Santa buttons from both the San Bernardino and Redlands stores. (Buttons courtesy of Steven Shaw and Aimmee Rodriguez.)

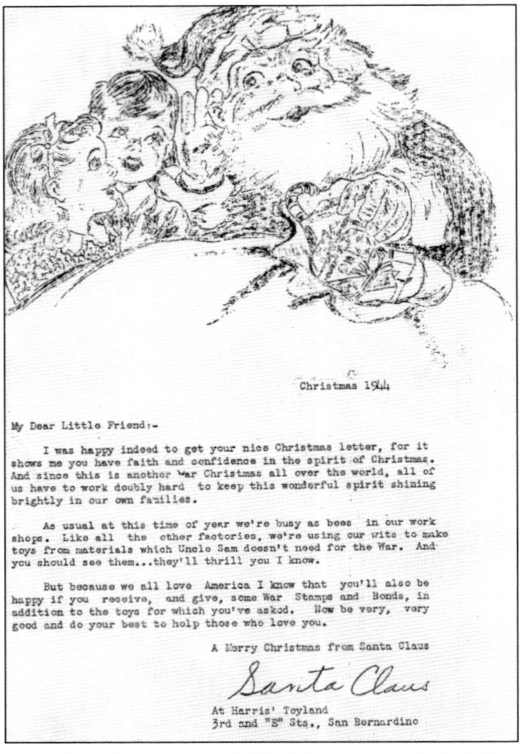

Christmas 1944

My Dear Little Friend:-

I was happy indeed to get your nice Christmas letter, for it shows me you have faith and confidence in the spirit of Christmas. And since this is another War Christmas all over the world, all of us have to work doubly hard to keep this wonderful spirit shining brightly in our own families.

As usual at this time of year we're busy as bees in our work shops. Like all the other factories, we're using our wits to make toys from materials which Uncle Sam doesn't need for the War. And you should see them...they'll thrill you I know.

But because we all love America I know that you'll also be happy if you receive, and give, some War Stamps and Bonds, in addition to the toys for which you've asked. Now be very, very good and do your best to help those who love you.

A Merry Christmas from Santa Claus

Santa Claus

At Harris' Toyland
3rd and "E" Sts., San Bernardino

HARRIS COMPANY SANTA LETTER, 1944. The Harris Company Santa letter in 1944 revealed the support the Harris Company had for the war effort. Because of rationing, Santa mentioned being innovative in creating toys from materials not needed for the war. He also encouraged customers to give and receive war stamps and bonds. At the 50th anniversary, the Harris Company reported that it had sold $2 million in war bonds.

SANTA CLAUS RECEIVES CHRISTMAS LETTERS, 1949. The arrival of Santa Claus for his month-long stay at the Harris Company Ice Palace and Toyland was greeted with fanfare. He arrived via helicopter to the cheers of thousands of children. He is pictured here at the National Orange Show accepting a bagful of Christmas letters with (from left to right) Leslie Harris, unidentified, and the postman.

SANTA PHOTOGRAPH CARDHOLDER, 1958. After children had their photograph taken with the Harris Company Santa, the image was placed in a cardholder. Pictured is a card from 1958 promoting the Harris Company San Bernardino and Riverside Photo Studios. On a present is the tagline in Christmas ribbon reading, "A Gift From Harris' Means More." (Courtesy of Michael Herring.)

MOCK-UP OF HARRIS' CHRISTMAS NEWSPAPER ADVERTISEMENT. The Harris Company had a team of talented artists, copywriters, and production people. Pictured here is a mock-up of a Harris Company Christmas advertisement with lines taken from *Let's Keep Christmas* by Peter Marshall. In 1968, Robert A. Sumpter was hired as the advertising manager and sales promotion coordinator. Under his guidance, the department won numerous newspaper-advertising awards.

EMPLOYEE MEETINGS. Once a month, store meetings were held in the Café Madrid, the Harris Company restaurant on the mezzanine level. The employees got to know all three Harris brothers, who treated them like family. The women's dress code was navy or black with hats and gloves in the winter, and white or gray in the summer, which many felt was classy.

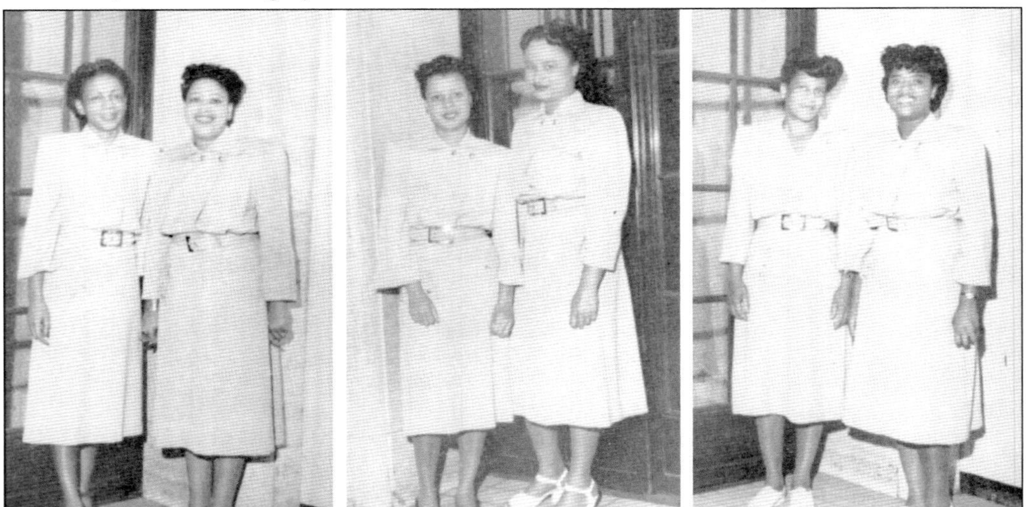

ELEVATOR OPERATORS, 1947. Though the motorstairs were installed in 1947, some customers were still wary of the contraption, and the needs of mothers who shopped with baby strollers could not be forgotten. Thus the elevator operators remained continually busy. Pictured here in new sand-colored fall uniforms are, from left to right, Ruby McAffee, Marie Jiggetts, Ouida Smallwood, May Kennedy, Bertha Fields, and Naomi Henderson.

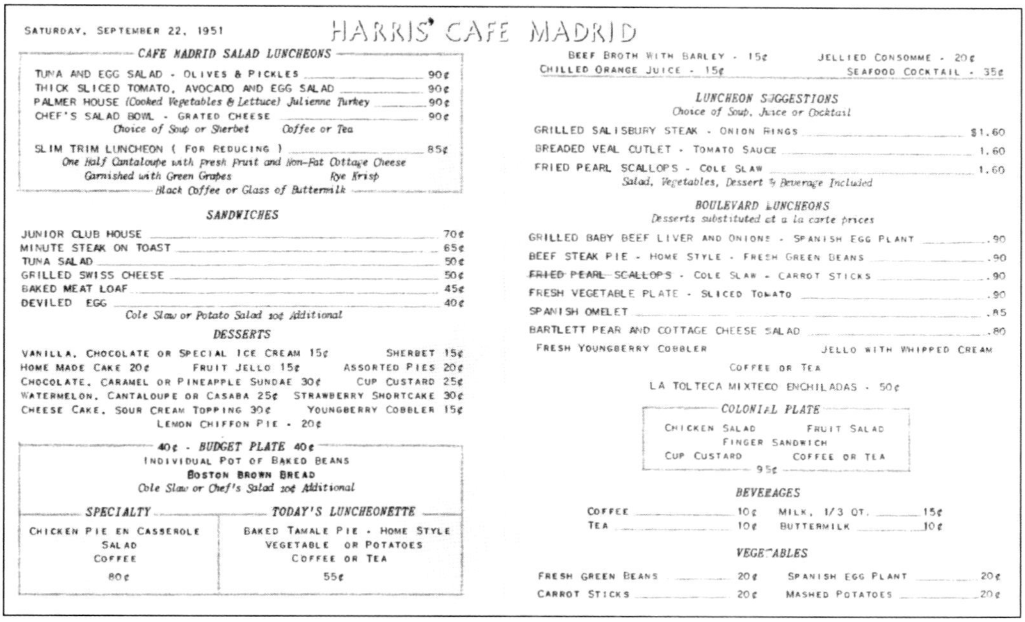

SATURDAY, SEPTEMBER 22, 1951

HARRIS' CAFE MADRID

CAFE MADRID SALAD LUNCHEONS

TUNA AND EGG SALAD - OLIVES & PICKLES .... 90¢
THICK SLICED TOMATO, AVOCADO AND EGG SALAD .... 90¢
PALMER HOUSE *(Cooked Vegetables & Lettuce) Julienne Turkey* .... 90¢
CHEF'S SALAD BOWL - GRATED CHEESE .... 90¢
Choice of Soup or Sherbet *Coffee or Tea*

SLIM TRIM LUNCHEON (FOR REDUCING) .... 85¢
One Half Cantaloupe with Fresh Fruit and Non-Fat Cottage Cheese
Garnished with Green Grapes *Rye Krisp*
Black Coffee or Glass of Buttermilk

SANDWICHES

JUNIOR CLUB HOUSE .... 70¢
MINUTE STEAK ON TOAST .... 65¢
TUNA SALAD .... 50¢
GRILLED SWISS CHEESE .... 50¢
BAKED MEAT LOAF .... 45¢
DEVILED EGG .... 40¢
Cole Slaw or Potato Salad 10¢ Additional

DESSERTS

VANILLA, CHOCOLATE OR SPECIAL ICE CREAM 15¢ SHERBET 15¢
HOME MADE CAKE 20¢ FRUIT JELLO 15¢ ASSORTED PIES 20¢
CHOCOLATE, CARAMEL OR PINEAPPLE SUNDAE 30¢ CUP CUSTARD 25¢
WATERMELON, CANTALOUPE OR CASABA 25¢ STRAWBERRY SHORTCAKE 30¢
CHEESE CAKE, SOUR CREAM TOPPING 30¢ YOUNGBERRY COBBLER 15¢
LEMON CHIFFON PIE - 20¢

40¢ - BUDGET PLATE 40¢
INDIVIDUAL POT OF BAKED BEANS
BOSTON BROWN BREAD
Cole Slaw or Chef's Salad 10¢ Additional

SPECIALTY
CHICKEN PIE EN CASSEROLE
SALAD
COFFEE
80¢

TODAY'S LUNCHEONETTE
BAKED TAMALE PIE - HOME STYLE
VEGETABLE OR POTATOES
COFFEE OR TEA
55¢

BEEF BROTH WITH BARLEY - 15¢ JELLIED CONSOMME - 20¢
CHILLED ORANGE JUICE - 15¢ SEAFOOD COCKTAIL - 35¢

LUNCHEON SUGGESTIONS
Choice of Soup, Juice or Cocktail

GRILLED SALISBURY STEAK - ONION RINGS $1.60
BREADED VEAL CUTLET - TOMATO SAUCE 1.60
FRIED PEARL SCALLOPS - COLE SLAW 1.60
Salad, Vegetables, Dessert & Beverage Included

BOULEVARD LUNCHEONS
Desserts substituted at a la carte prices

GRILLED BABY BEEF LIVER AND ONIONS - SPANISH EGG PLANT .... .90
BEEF STEAK PIE - HOME STYLE - FRESH GREEN BEANS .... .90
~~FRIED PEARL~~ SCALLOPS - COLE SLAW - CARROT STICKS .... .90
FRESH VEGETABLE PLATE - SLICED TOMATO .... .90
SPANISH OMELET .... .85
BARTLETT PEAR AND COTTAGE CHEESE SALAD .... .80
FRESH YOUNGBERRY COBBLER JELLO WITH WHIPPED CREAM
COFFEE OR TEA

LA TOLTECA MIXTECO ENCHILADAS - 50¢

COLONIAL PLATE
CHICKEN SALAD FRUIT SALAD
FINGER SANDWICH
CUP CUSTARD COFFEE OR TEA
95¢

BEVERAGES

COFFEE .... 10¢ MILK, 1/3 QT. .... 15¢
TEA .... 10¢ BUTTERMILK .... 10¢

VEGETABLES

FRESH GREEN BEANS .... 20¢ SPANISH EGG PLANT .... 20¢
CARROT STICKS .... 20¢ MASHED POTATOES .... 20¢

CAFÉ MADRID MENU, 1951. One customer remembered dining at the café as a teenager for the best tacos around. Another recalled as a little girl, having to be on her best behavior when visiting the restaurant. With its ornately decorated beamed ceiling, it was the perfect place for ladies to wear their white gloves and hats, have tea or coffee, enjoy a trip to town, or a respite from shopping. (Courtesy of Aimmee Rodriguez.)

CAFÉ MADRID KITCHEN CREW, 1947. The kitchen staff worked hard and under pressure to time all they did. Yet they still smiled, and occasionally even a song could be heard. The buying public and employees agreed that the employees made the Café Madrid a good place to eat. Pictured here from left to right are (first row) Tolly Taylor, Hattie Holloway, and Billie Nelson; (second row) Angelo Flores, Joe Fugate, and Ralph Williams.

EMPLOYEE CHRISTMAS BREAKFAST. Harris' employees always felt they had a job for life and benefited from management's personal relationship with them. The Harris Company usually hired music and entertainment from Los Angeles, such as Rosemary Clooney, for the annual Christmas breakfasts. Pictured here are top employees with members of the Harris family. From left to right are Leslie, Arthur, unidentified, George Waterfall, Bertha Tebo, unidentified, Harold, Lillian Eldridge, and Melville.

THE HARRIS COMPANY TAILORS, 1951. The Harris Company prided itself on quality. Experienced tailors upheld customers' high expectations. Foreman Frank Czuk (left) had his own shop in Hungary and taught the tailoring trade in a night school. Fred Ruffolo (center) came from Chicago in 1921 and worked for numerous fine shops in Los Angeles. Finally, Lee Szachtus (right) worked as a tailor for many years in Munchen, Germany, before arriving in 1949.

BALI HAI LUNCHROOM. Bali Hai on the fourth floor was for the exclusive use of the Harris Company employees. It served lunch and, when the store was open late, dinner. If employees brought their own food, they were encouraged to eat in the employee lunchroom or the Sun Deck (roof), which was accessible through a stairway in Bali Hai.

HARRIS' BUDGET FURNITURE STORE, 1949. The Harris Company opened a budget furniture store on February 14, 1949, south of the main store. Harris' management wanted customers to experience a higher standard of living by providing the convenience of home appliances without the burden of straining their budgets. Junior, a General Electric refrigerator and home freezer that walked and talked, was present for the store's opening. (Courtesy of the San Bernardino County Museum.)

Harris Company Display Window, 1955. The Harris Company celebrated its 50th anniversary by telling its history through displays. As stated in the sign, this window showcased the "most fashionable modes worn by Harris' patrons in 1905" and encouraged customers to come in and see the various exhibits throughout the store.

Gingerbread Rendition of Harris' First Location, 1955. Isabel Taylor and George Waterfall of the Harris Company Food Services made a model of Harris' first store in the old Armory Building. The gingerbread structure was revealed at the Old-Timers Reception on the fourth floor as part of the 50th anniversary celebration.

REPLICA OF HARRIS' INTERIOR, 1955. The Harris Company transformed its fourth floor into a museum for the golden anniversary celebration. Turn-of-the-century swimsuits, clothing, millinery, modes of transportation, and a barbershop were exhibited. The feature display was a replica of a portion of the Harris Company's first store. The "old-timers," employees who had been with the company for 25 years or more, were dressed in period costumes. Pictured here from left to right are Leslie Harris, Melville Harris, Dorothea Brogan, Florence Spezzi, unidentified, and Hazel Swanson.

Employee Gift to the Harris Company Founders, 1955. At the opening of the Harris Company department store in 1927, the 121 employees dedicated a beautifully ornate, four-dial clock as a tribute to the founders' courage and perseverance in bringing to the community a shopping place quite beyond expectation. It was not uncommon to hear the phrase, "Meet me under the clock." This photograph was taken during the 50th anniversary celebration.

Golden Anniversary Sale, April 1955. Anniversary sales were always big events at the Harris Company. For the 50th anniversary, the bargain sales lasted from April 19 through April 30. Each day had a theme, such as Opening Day, Founders Day, Golden Opportunity Day, Last Three Days, and Final 'Best Yet' Day. The night before the sale began for the public, the Harris Company closed early to allow the employees to take advantage of the great values.

S&H GREEN STAMPS, 1958. S&H Green Stamps were a regular part of the shopping experience at the Harris Company. Each purchase would allow a customer a certain amount of stamps. Collected over time, completed stamp books gave customers an opportunity to trade books for various items or prizes in a special catalogue. Pictured here is the Harris Company tower advertising "We Give S&H Green Stamps." (Courtesy of the San Bernardino County Museum.)

S&H LUNCHEON, 1965. Redeeming S&H Green Stamps was part of the Harris Company since its early days in San Bernardino. At the company's 60th anniversary celebration, representatives from the Sperry and Hutchinson Company held a special luncheon for Harris Company department store officials. Mayors, government officials, publishers, and other dignitaries from three metropolitan areas joined to honor the Harris family for their success and contributions to the Inland Empire.

SODA FOUNTAIN, 1949. Originally located on the main floor, then later moved to the mezzanine level after the motorstair remodel, the soda fountain was a hit. Teens could purchase a sundae or a huge banana split for 17¢ with their Harris Company Teen Club card. Pictured here are Bob Botts and Joyce Gallatin of San Bernardino enjoying ice cream sodas.

THE HARRIS COMPANY ORGANIST, 1958. During the summer months of 1958 and 1959, Carol Bunting, a student at San Bernardino High School, played the organ for the Harris Company. Her father actually rented a truck to transport the family's Hammond organ to the store. From the mezzanine level, Carol entertained many shoppers.

CANDY SHOP. When the Harris Company department store first opened in 1927, the candy counter, located on the first floor, included a bakery. Later, after the store was remodeled for the motorstairs, the glass-enclosed candy counter was moved to the mezzanine level. One customer said her child thought that was where the Easter bunny purchased all of his goods.

FURNITURE DEPARTMENT. Located on the third floor after the escalators were installed, the entrance to the furniture department looked as if one were entering a home. Fine furniture, rugs, lamps, and draperies were featured. Arthur Rutherfurd, who previously owned Rutherfurd Maple Shop, was hired to open and manage the department.

CAMPUS DEB SHOP, 1962. One of the Harris Company's many community commitments was to the high schools in the region. The company bought advertisement space in the yearly annuals and hosted teen fashion shows, sponsored teen clubs, and elected a teen board. Campus Debs played an important part in the lives of Inland Empire teens. One remembered during her sophomore year that she and her girlfriend sought just the right sweater for their senior-year pictures.

CAMPUS DEBS ADVERTISEMENT, 1953. A few times a year, the Harris Company would put on a fashion show featuring student models, special drawings, and a movie specifically for teens. Entertainment included local bands and sometimes well-known acts such as the Torquays, whose theme for the movie *Endless Summer* became a classic surfer anthem. One year, the show was held in the California Theater after it outgrew the Harris Company auditorium.

BMOC ADVERTISEMENT, 1964. BMOC stood for "Big Man On Campus." Only the coolest clothes were sold in Harris' Varsity Shop for the valley's young men. Pictured here from left to right are (top) Curt Bailey, BMOC Eisenhower High School; and Sam Gabriel, BMOC San Bernardino High; (middle) Richard Migala, BMOC Fontana High; and Roger Morris, BMOC Pacific High; (bottom) George Rigney, BMOC Aquinas High; and Dennis Zane, BMOC Colton Union High. (Courtesy of Sam Gabriel.)

CAMPUS DEB AND BMOC REPRESENTATIVES, 1967. Every year, the Harris Company would select a fashionable boy and girl from each of the local high schools to be on the teen board, work part time, and represent the Campus Deb and Varsity Shop departments at store events. Pictured here are San Bernardino High School's Campus Deb, Janis Findlay, and BMOC, Matthew Stuart.

DOWNTOWN REDEVELOPMENT, LATE 1960S. The suburbs grew steadily after World War II, and along with a spurt of highway construction across America, old downtowns suffered. San Bernardino, like many cities, succumbed to developers, losing huge swaths of historic structures. Saved were the Harris Company (above left) and the Andreson Building, both constructed in 1927 by Howard E. Jones. Between the two structures, arches can be seen for the new Central City Mall, completed in 1973. The rear façades of the buildings are pictured below. Just months before his death, Leslie Harris stated, "we like nothing better than to go up on our roof and see what is going on all over. Our greatest thrill is seeing our downtown rebuilt." Third Street, running between the buildings, was removed, and the buildings near Harris' were razed. (Above, courtesy of the San Bernardino County Museum.)

Strengthening the Building, Late 1960s. As the new mall was being built, the Harris Company used this time to bring the building up to code. Pictured above, old floors were taken out, and the entire structure was retrofitted to meet up-to-date earthquake standards. The top of the motorstairs can be seen on the right. Pictured below is the main floor just inside the main entrance. The majority of the mezzanine level was removed. Café Madrid, gift-wrapping, and altering facilities remained, and executive offices were moved to the fourth floor that was built in 1947.

A Last Look at the Windows, Late 1960s. Of all the changes happening downtown, the decision to infill the windows of the Harris building altered its look forever. The needs of the department store changed, and with walls instead of windows, display space increased throughout the store.

Making a South Entrance, Late 1960s. Just south of the Harris Company was the Harris Annex, formerly Sage's Market. When this structure was removed, a new south entrance was constructed. The windows on the south façade were also infilled, and new details were used to draw attention to this area. An arch was created as a simpler version of the grand entrance on the north side of the building.

CONNECTION TO MALL, 1982. When the Central City Mall was constructed in the early 1970s, its first and second floors were offset from the Harris Company's first and second floor. The Harris Company redesign team used tiles and wrought iron from Portugal to create a beautiful stairway and landing in order to create a link to the mall. They moved the ornate ceiling clock from its original location on the main floor to the new staircase to complete the space. This photograph shows the stairway decorated for the Christmas season.

The Company During the Recession, 1970s. The Harris Company embarked on an ambitious expansion and modernization plan just as the American economy fell into a recession. Cash-flow problems resulted, and for the first time in its history, Harris' laid off nearly 40 percent of its staff. Departments such as the record, toy, and lending library were closed. Pictured here from left to right are Hap, Don, and Melville Harris. (Courtesy of Joan H. Hall.)

The Harris Company Welcomes El Corté Inglés, 1982. In the late 1970s, the Harris Company began looking for partners of a family business similar to theirs. El Corté Inglés, Spain's largest retailer, purchased controlling interest in the Harris Company in the early 1980s. Pictured here is the front of the welcome luncheon program with Servimus, "We Serve," under the Harris family coat-of-arms.

JORGE PONT. Jorge was named president and chief executive officer of Harris' in February 1982. El Corté Inglés and the Harris Company shared the philosophy of treating the customers with courtesy. Pont studied the Harris Approach and was determined to bring personal service back to the company.

EXTERIOR OF HARRIS', 1988. The new owners improved Harris' presentation by relocating storerooms and offices. They managed to utilize an additional 4,500 square feet of selling space on the first floor alone. Pictured here is the exterior of the building that shows the results of the 1960s downtown redevelopment. Though still interesting, the richness of the building's architecture was lost in the monochromatic color scheme. (Courtesy of the San Bernardino County Museum.)

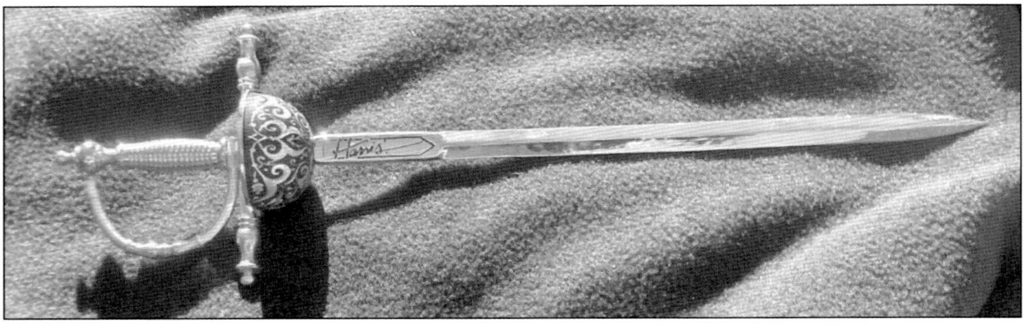

HARRIS' LETTER OPENER, 1999. When El Corté Inglés took over Harris' in the early 1980s, the new management gave each Harris family member an intricately detailed letter opener. The letter opener was a miniature version of swords made in Spain with Harris' engraved on the hilt. This specialty item was reserved for unique occasions, such as fashion show fund-raisers, and was not available for sale in the store. (Courtesy of Aimmee Rodriguez.)

BUYING THE BUILDING. In 1980, Harris' sold the building to Carcorp Financial Incorporated of Beverly Hills for $9.5 million but leased the building for 30 years. This was a common transaction for companies wanting equity for expansions and improvements. In 1994, Harris' management sought loans to buy the building back and the land beneath it. Marconi Management owned the land and planned to increase the lease in 1995 to $700,000. (Courtesy of Aimmee Rodriguez.)

ARCHITECTURAL DETAILS OF THE HARRIS BUILDING, 2001. Harris' committed to renovating the San Bernardino store after receiving loans from the Department of Housing and Urban Development and from the City of San Bernardino in 1996. Pictured here is the stonework and the Harris coat-of-arms painted in dark gray, the grillwork in contemporary purple, and the building in a light neutral tone. (Courtesy of Aimmee Rodriguez.)

SOUTH ENTRANCE. As part of the renovations, the south entrance received a facelift in 1996. The arch over the south entrance that was constructed in the late 1960s was removed. In its place, new tiles and architectural details gave prominence to the south façade of the building. (Courtesy of Aimmee Rodriguez.)

THE LAST DECADES, 2001. Harris' survived the redevelopment of the 1960s, but plans to expand the chain and to upgrade computer systems as the country moved into a recession had far-reaching effects. Parent company El Corté Inglés stepped in and helped to grow the chain to nine stores. When loans were sought in the mid-1990s, the community and city leadership banded together to ensure Harris' stayed in business. Federal loans that usually take six months for approval passed in a record seven weeks. Yet America experienced another recession, and the closing of Norton Air Force Base in 1994 further devastated the local economy. American shopping trends shifted. Competition with stores such as Target, Marshalls, and Ross made consolidation with the Gottschalks chain in 1998 critical for survival. With a new Gottschalks store recently built a few miles south at Inland Center Mall, the merger resulted in the closing of the flagship store in San Bernardino on January 31, 1999. The remaining eight stores became Harris Gottschalks. El Corté Inglés retained ownership of the building and the name the Harris Company. (Courtesy of Aimmee Rodriguez.)

Three

THE HARRIS COMPANY IN REDLANDS

NEW STOREFRONT IN REDLANDS, CALIFORNIA, 1926. From the ashes, the new Harris Company of Redlands opened to great fanfare on March 8, 1926. The two-story structure had a front of rouge-colored brick decorated with diamond tracings and tile work. Italian marble lined the base of the display windows leading to the entrance—solid mahogany doors with brass hinges.

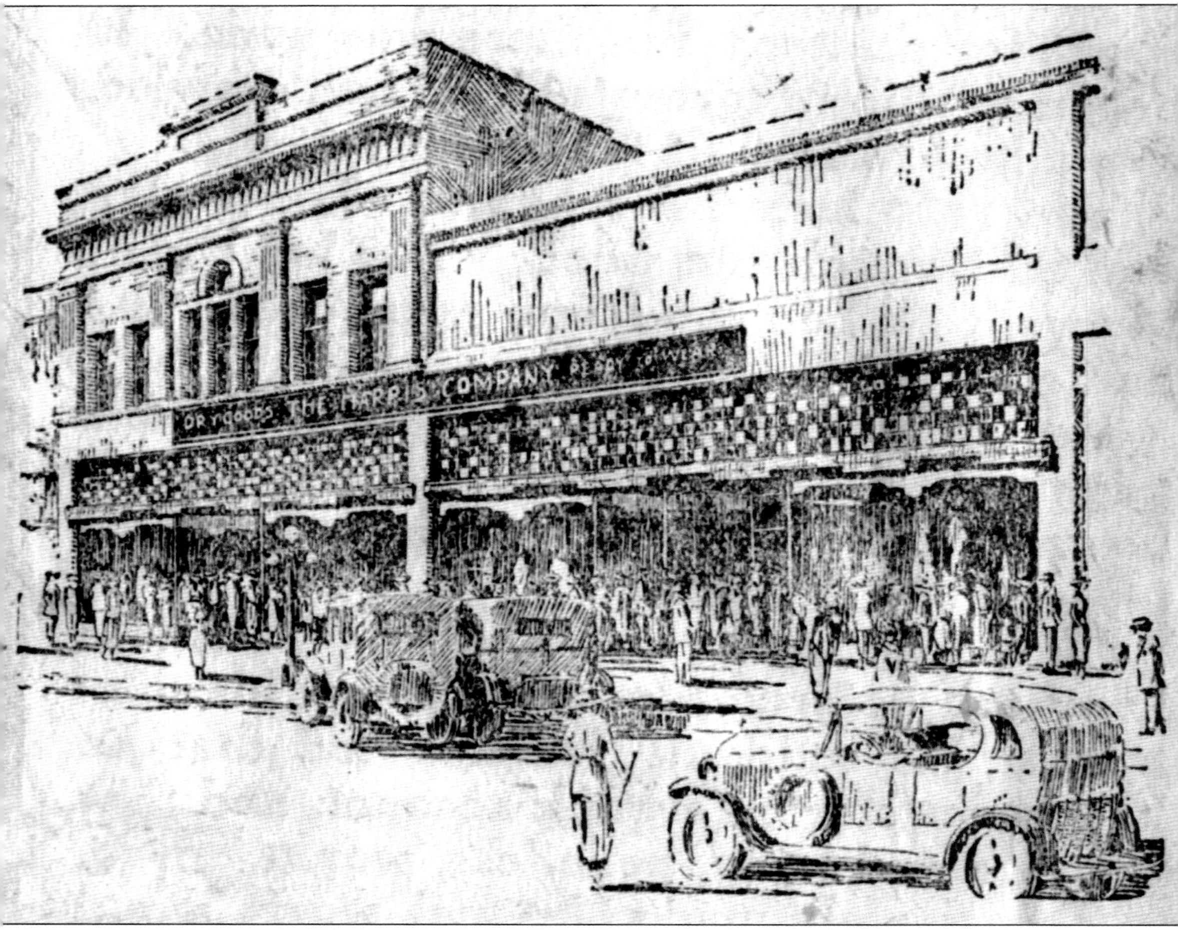

SKETCH OF STATE STREET IN REDLANDS, CALIFORNIA, 1922. The Harris brothers opened their second store in Redlands in 1908 with the purchase of the dry-goods store of Randall and Merriman located at 217 Orange Street. Philip Harris moved to Redlands the next year and managed that store until his death in 1939. Success prompted a move in 1915 for more space to 17 East State Street. Another expansion four years later gave the store 135 feet of frontage of "variously designed buildings." Disaster struck in 1925 when fire swept through the store, taking with it an estimated $120,000 in stock. Undaunted by the loss, Herman Harris reportedly took charge "even as flames were still licking at the remains." Trucks were dispatched to San Bernardino and Los Angeles, and new stock was brought to Redlands. Philip Harris immediately leased the nearby Parker Building, and the residents of Redlands rallied to his assistance. University of Redlands' students aided employees in decorating the temporary quarters, which opened successfully, if slightly cramped, the next day. "A store hadn't just burned down," stated a daily newspaper. "Friends and neighbors were in trouble."

EXTERIOR VIEW

STORE IN REDLANDS, CALIFORNIA, 1926. The store held "a pervasive sense of mahogany," according to one report. Inside the patio effect was highlighted by a second floor mezzanine augmented by the diffuse rays of a light well above, which produced a sense of loftiness and coolness.

INTERIOR VIEW

A Booster Pamphlet for the Harris Puppets, Redlands, California, 1940s. In a cross between promotional genius and civic entertainment, the Harris family found puppetry to be a family activity that resonated with friends and members of the public of all ages.

AN EFFECTIVE PLAN

WE PRESENT AN EFFECTIVE PLAN to raise money for your activities budget.

But first listen to our own experience that you may better appreciate the merits of this offer.

The Assistance League of Redlands needed funds for a new Welfare Project. The Harrises offered the services of their famous puppet troupe for a series of entertainments to raise the budget, and what happened? . . . In two engagements, four hundred precious, sparkling dollars rolled in, painlessly and leaving only the pleasantest of memories. NOW—through the generosity of this talented family, the money-earning ability of this splendid troupe is yours for the asking!

The offer is purely a co-operative one. It is an ideal money-raising project for Parent-Teachers Associations, Hospital Auxiliaries, Junior Leagues, Aid Societies, Church Groups, Luncheon Clubs and similar organizations within a radius of one hundred miles of Redlands.

It is simply this . . . The Harris Puppets will come to your city under your organization's sponsorship if you feel you can insure a reasonable audience. No guarantees required! You share the net proceeds on a fifty-fifty basis with the Assistance League of Redlands. You take no risks! You simply cannot lose. The Harris Puppet Troupe is the one project

THAT GETS RESULTS

"If you haven't seen Egbert . . . you don't know what entertainment is."
ED AINSWORTH, *Los Angeles Times.*

"I had lots of fun Saturday . . . I went to see the Harris Marionettes."
MARGARET STEEN, *Riverside Press-Enterprise.*

"Another financial success was scored by the Assistance League as a result of the Harris Puppets."
WINIFRED MARTIN, *San Bernardino Sun.*

"They hiss the villan, they applaud the hero, they stomp their feet, they laugh . . . !
MARION WALKER, *Redlands Daily Facts*

"Remarkable little caricatures that come to life."
BRUCE RUSSELL, *Cartoonist, Los Angeles Times.*

"Life-like facial movements give these puppets true dramatic fervor."
VICTOR JORY, *Eighteen Actors, Inc., Pasadena*

THE HARRISES

and Their Fascinating Marionettes

Harold, Jeanette, Harriet and Happy do virtually nothing except run a successful business in Redlands, maintain perpetual open house, go to school, write plays, and design, model and manipulate puppets that make Hollywood stars look like candle flickers. Puppetry is the family hobby, however; and when the Harrises realized how much fun their plays gave to others also, they had a new and generous idea. They offered themselves and their puppets as an entertainment unit to organizations which wished to raise funds for community service. They like nothing better than to pack a station wagon full of stuff & things, and drive a hundred miles to perform for an audience that is supporting charitable, child welfare and other worthwhile local activities.

Their puppets have created a new standard of puppetry through the use of intricate facial maneuvers. Reginald Egbert Simp as Master of Ceremonies presides with floating eyebrows and roving eyes, the villain smiles with fiendish glee as the heroine drops her eyelids in remorse and her brother wiggles his ears. You'll like these people.

THIS IS WHAT WE DO

The Assistance League will supply all stag and scenic effects, music and sound equipment lights and necessary talent for a one and a half hour performance, the like of which will mak young and old split their differences with genuin laughter and hearty approval.

The program will include a now famous Harri mellerdrammer, "At the Old Cross Roads." No just an ordinary mellerdrammer, but one so impressive, so convincing that it will leave its benevolent blessings on the ego for the rest of you taxable days. In addition your customers will se a ten act olio with over thirty star performers Their life-like expressions and animated antics hav not been surpassed in the entire realm of puppetry All of them are gems of wit and humor. The Glo Worm Dance, with 12-year old Harriet Harris a the strings, is so real in time and technique, s heart-rending, so beautifully accomplished that i will squeeze the last remaining dollar out of the most impenetrable pinchfist.

The Assistance League and the Harrises will giv as many evening performances as are necessary t accommodate the crowds, be there one, two o three. We will give a special children's matinee We will work hard with coats peeled off an sleeves rolled up that YOUR and OUR Welfar Funds may be enriched.

THIS IS WHAT YOU DO

The Harris Puppet Project is so complete i every detail that there is little left for you to do Simply have a responsible officer of your organization fill out the attached coupon. Be sure to reques a tentative billing date so that one may be reserve for you on our schedule. Upon receipt of you request we will promptly send you more specifi information.

Remember! No guarantee is required when yo share the net receipts with the Assistance Leagu of Redlands. Should you prefer other arrangements, our Director of Puppet Troupe will co operate in any way possible.

Busy holidays are ahead . . . the right time t raise money for under-privileged children. So "u on your toes" . . . do not delay! Fill out and ma the attached coupon today!

The ASSISTANCE LEAGUE OF REDLANDS

A Booster Pamphlet, Redlands, California, 1940s. Harris family puppet shows—"The Harrises and Their Fascinating Marionettes"—were advertised in a booster pamphlet of the Assistance League of Redlands. "They like nothing better than to pack a station wagon full of stuff & things, and drive a hundred miles to perform for an audience that is supporting charitable, child welfare and other worthwhile local activities," read the pamphlet.

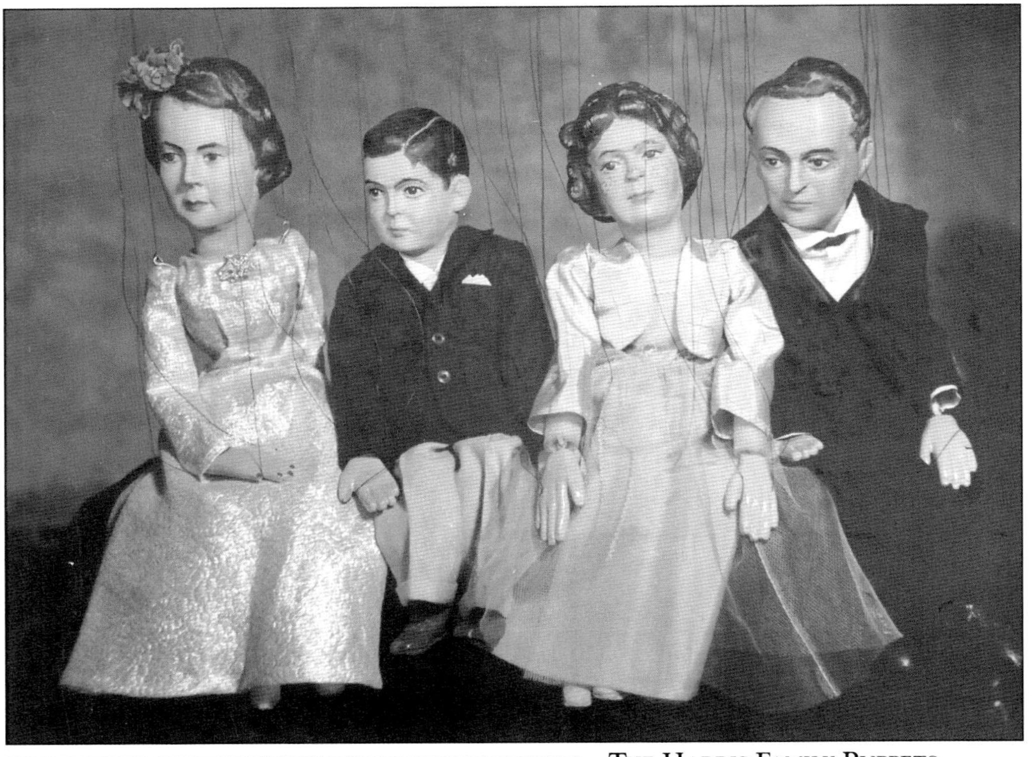

The Harris Family Puppets, Redlands, California, 1940s. For Jeanette and Harold Harris Sr. and their children Harriet and Harold "Hap" Jr., puppetry was a family hobby. Starting in the late 1930s, the family crafted the marionettes from clay, plaster, and wood dough, creating roughly 30 characters ranging from circus performers, tap dancers, and even precise replicas of the family members themselves, as shown above.

Hap Harris and His Puppet, Redlands, California, 1942. Nine-year-old "Hap" Harris poses with his personal look-alike. What started as family fun soon attracted the praise of friends and, eventually, offers to perform the shows to raise funds for civic organizations and community service. Groups such as the Redlands Assistance League, child welfare agencies, and the USO during World War II benefited from the entertaining presentations.

A BALLERINA PUPPET, REDLANDS, CALIFORNIA, 1940S. The dresses and costumes were designed professionally for the puppets, and some of the wigs were created by the hairdresser for the famous Russian ballerina Anna Pavlova. Young Harriet Harris' string dexterity during the Glo-Worm Dance is reported to have been a particular crowd-pleaser.

THE MASTER OF CEREMONY PUPPET, REDLANDS, CALIFORNIA, 1940S. Family members wrote the scripts for the puppet shows and performed all the voices. The master of ceremonies was Reginald Egbert Simp, shown here. The marionettes were known for intricate facial maneuvers, such as Reginald's floating eyebrows and roving eyes.

STREET SCENE OF THE HARRIS COMPANY IN REDLANDS, APRIL 1948. The building on the far left in this picture is the La Posada Hotel of Redlands, which was at the corner of State and Orange Streets. Hotel operations ceased in the late 1960s, and the building was demolished in 1976 to make way for the Redlands Mall. Notice that the Harris Company's facade is now painted white. (Courtesy Adair Photography, collection of the late William Elmer Kingham.)

STOREFRONT OF THE HARRIS COMPANY IN REDLANDS, CALIFORNIA. Pictured is the Harris Company at 17–23 State Street as it appeared in the 1950s. Visible in the second window from the right is one of the first televisions marketed in the United States. (Courtesy Adair Photography, collection of the late William Elmer Kingham.)

Window Displays for the 50th Anniversary of The Harris Company in Redlands, California, 1955. Harris stores celebrated their 50 years of service by creating display windows that featured nostalgic fashion of the eras in which they played such an important part in the Inland Empire.

DOLLAR DAYS AT THE HARRIS COMPANY IN REDLANDS, CALIFORNIA, 1958. Eager shoppers queue up early on August 8, 1958, to take advantage of "Dollar Days." This yearly event had been recently merged with "Back to School Days" to create the bargain event of the year. Stores throughout western San Bernardino County joined in with promotions and additional staff for this new slant that offered greater savings.

DRESS SHOP AND HAIR SALON IN THE HARRIS COMPANY, REDLANDS, CALIFORNIA, 1962. The Harris Company was a one-stop shop for the busy housewife or college student. From contemporary dress fashions to state-of-the-art hair salons, a customer could get a compete makeover at the Harris stores. The "open hair styling" motif was a new innovation in beauty salons. Sheldon Rothstein managed Harris' salons for approximately 20 years.

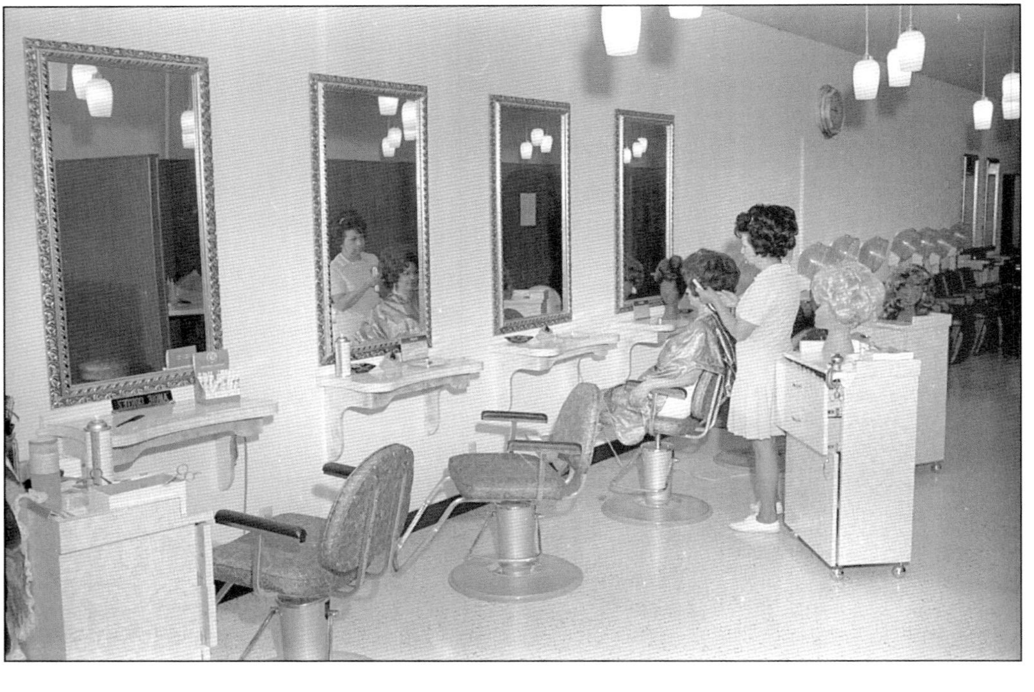

SALESPEOPLE HELPING CUSTOMERS IN THE HARRIS COMPANY, REDLANDS, CALIFORNIA, 1966. The Harris Company was known for its caring and accommodating staff. Judi Mosby, who started with the company in 1969, remembered that it was always about the people. According to Mosby, the Harris stores had "a family atmosphere," and "each store was like a mini family."

THE HARRIS COMPANY IN REDLANDS DURING THE DIAMOND JUBILEE CELEBRATION, 1963. Harold Harris (center) and company employees gather in front of the Harris store during citywide festivities celebrating the 75th anniversary of the incorporation of Redlands. All are dressed in garb depicting the late 1880s.

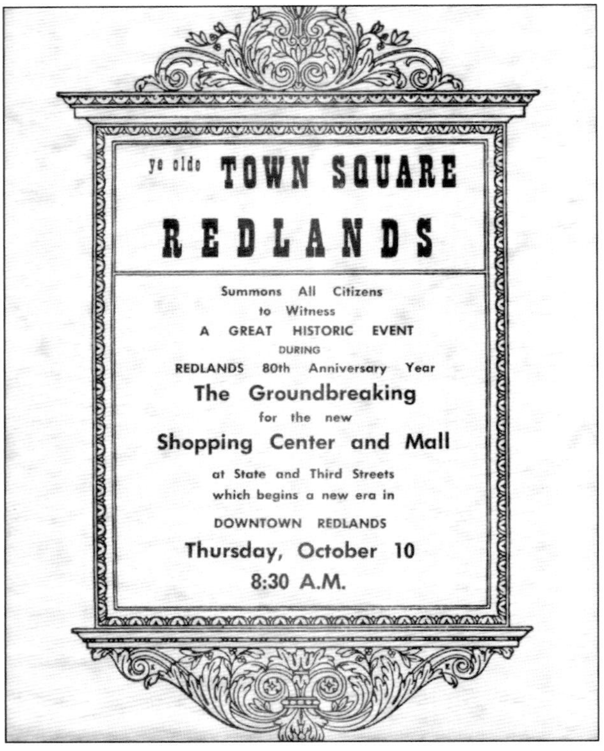

ADVERTISEMENT FOR THE NEW SHOPPING CENTER AND MALL IN REDLANDS, CALIFORNIA, 1977. In 1977, the Harris Company moved its State Street store to the new Redlands Mall, where it became the anchor tenet for the 200,000-square-foot development. Throughout the Harris Company history, the Redlands store always boasted strong numbers, even through the merger with Gottschalks.

HAROLD HARRIS JR. AND PEGGY WILLIAMS AT REDLANDS HARRIS GOTTSCHALKS, MARCH 13, 2001. Outside of the internal entrance to the Redlands store, "Hap" Harris and assistant manager Peggy Williams pose under the new sign of Harris Gottschalks following the sale of the store to the Fresno-based chain. Ironically, Gottschalks was started in 1904 by German immigrant Emil Gottschalk with a motto of "the store that cares," a background and philosophy which mirrored that of the Harris brothers. (Courtesy of Aimmee Rodriguez.)

WALL PAINTINGS IN THE HARRIS COMPANY, REDLANDS, CALIFORNIA, 2007. A favorite fashion period for department manager Jana McIver was the late 1950s and early 1960s. She asked fellow manager Aubrey Robin to re-create period advertisements of that time on the walls of her office at the Harris Gottschalks of Redlands. (Courtesy of Aimmee Rodriguez.)

More Wall Paintings in the Harris Company, Redlands, California, 2007. "I love fashion," said McIver, "It's who I am." These particular advertisements were special to her, she said. McIver moved up the corporate ladder to the Hemet store, leaving the drawings she loved. They were painted over in 2007. (Courtesy of Aimmee Rodriguez.)

Four

THE HARRIS COMPANY IN RIVERSIDE

OPENING CEREMONY OF HARRIS' RIVERSIDE, SEPTEMBER 30, 1957. Never was there a more brilliant and impressive ceremony than the grand opening of the Harris Company in Riverside. Several thousand people came to show their respect and appreciation for the founders and heirs of this organization, who had consistently been mindful of civic, cultural, and progressive advancement.

THREE HARRIS BROTHERS UPHOLD LONG TRADITION IN RIVERSIDE, CALIFORNIA, 1957. The second generation of Harris brothers, Leslie, Melville, and Harold, stroll below along the plaza, determined to make their new Riverside store a leader in its field. The building, pictured above, was one of the tallest buildings in the city in 1957 and was an impressive addition to the Riverside landscape. These brothers revealed a quiet pride in the mercantile traditions developed through four generations of service to Southern California shoppers. "We work as a team," said Harold. "Each of us is different, and each does the kind of work for which he is best suited. That is one of the advantages of these close family ties. We have our difference of opinion, of course, but there is no jealousy, no fear somebody is trying to get our job, no empire building." Another advantage is the kind of loyalty that grows out of the realization that not only is your financial welfare dependent on the success of your business, but your own reputation and even your self-respect are inextricably linked with what people think of your store.

FLAG-RAISING FORMALITY FOR HARRIS' RIVERSIDE, SEPTEMBER 30, 1957. The functional flag-raising occasion was one of special significance to the Harris family because it denoted an important milestone in the career of the merchants, first of whom was Morris Harris, a great lover of freedom, who fled to the United States in the 1840s.

THE HARRIS COMPANY'S FIRST EMPLOYEE. William Engel, manager of Harris' Riverside, introduced Mabel Swanson Reeves as one of the company's first employees, having started with the Harris Company in 1905.

The Ribbon-Cutting Ceremony at Harris' Riverside, September 30, 1957. People anxiously await the ribbon cutting, which would formally open the new Riverside store.

Crowds Enter Harris' Riverside After the Ceremony, September 30, 1957. Shoppers crowd through the front doors following the official opening. Mrs. Philip (Leah) Harris, matriarch of the family, cut the ribbon.

OPENING DAY IN THE JEWELRY DEPARTMENT AT HARRIS' RIVERSIDE, SEPTEMBER 30, 1957. Many customers, mostly women, visited the jewelry department and the candy shop.

Appreciative Letter From From Child Welfare Chairman

Dear Mr. Gottlieb:

This is such a few words to say a real big "Thank You" to you and your co-workers for all the lovely things for children in Sanitariums and Camps. Th- petticoats are used for the Indian girls and I am also going to take some to Hipass for the children in Camp to use in their plays.

Used greeting cards are used to amuse tiny tots—the older children make place cards and gift enclosures. Jewelry is sorted—good pieces are given to the girls as is., and broken jewelry is used in arts and crafts. Old hosiery is used to stuff dolls. Clothing for small children is taken to the sanitoriums. Thanks so much.

Esther Rubidart
Child Welfare Chairman
Los Angeles County No. 32

Perhaps you may have talent or aptitude for an interesting hobby. Frequently a hobby has been known to develop into a very lucrative business.

Pictured Beneath Is The "Coty Girl" Doll

Just as you have been seeing her on TV. This exquisite doll has the exclusive designed hat and gown fashioned by "Lily Dache."

She is a very beautiful 10½ inch "Full Formed Doll" with high heels and many exquisite gowns.

Also included is a pearl necklace, pearl drop earrings, pearl bracelet, black felt hat, nylon stockings and shoes. What a wonderful Chrismas gift for your little darling, or her pal.

Please be advised, the toy department in our three stores are ready to serve you with, we believe, the largest selections of wonderful toys outside the metropolitan southland. We will be happy to serve you—and your many frinds.

"Life is real! Life is earnest and the grave is not it's goal. Dust thou art, to dust returnest, was spoken of the soul."—Longfellow

Technology plus the free enterprise system has tripled the output per man-hour of America's working force since the turn of the century.

THE HARRIS BOOSTER NEWS Page 15

ADVERTISEMENT FOR 1957 COTY GIRL DOLL. This Coty cosmetics advertising doll, all vinyl, measuring 10.5 inches tall, with sleep eyes, rooted hair of various colors, high heels, and pierced ears, was shown wearing the exclusive designed hat and gown fashioned by "Lily Dache."

OPENING DAY IN WOMEN'S ACCESSORIES AT HARRIS' RIVERSIDE, SEPTEMBER 30, 1957. Customers loved the open style and self selection fixtures on the street floor in the new store.

DEDICATION OF THE CLOCK IN HARRIS', RIVERSIDE, CALIFORNIA, NOVEMBER 1957. The Harris Booster Club presented Leslie Harris with the beautiful, black, metal, four-faced clock, pictured here hanging from the ceiling on the street floor.

OPENING DAY IN WOMEN'S WEAR AT HARRIS' RIVERSIDE, SEPTEMBER 30, 1957. Crowds continued to explore the store as they made their way to the second floor to find all kinds of new and wonderful merchandise.

OPENING DAY IN THE LAYETTE SHOP AT HARRIS' RIVERSIDE, SEPTEMBER 30, 1957. Women loved looking at the delicate merchandise in the layette shop and looked forward to using the photo studio.

PRESS PARTY FOR THE GRAND OPENING, HARRIS' RIVERSIDE, SEPTEMBER 1957. Following traditional policies, a press party was held, and section managers assumed the duties of tour guides for the new building. Champagne punch with hors d'oeuvres was served to the guests.

ARTIST'S RENDERING OF HARRIS' RIVERSIDE, 1957. This artist's rendering of the new store in Riverside was used on the cover of the *Harris Booster News*, an informative multipage newsletter published by and for the employees of the Harris Company.

HARRIS' IN THE RIVERSIDE PLAZA, RIVERSIDE, CALIFORNIA, 1957. The Harris store was the keystone of the Riverside Plaza development, and the plaza, in turn, was the new kind of suburban, one-stop shopping center attuned to the new kind of suburban living.

COMMUNITY BENEVOLENCE DAY AT THE HARRIS COMPANY IN RIVERSIDE, CALIFORNIA, MARCH 18, 1958. The Norwegian blue stole, which Mrs. P. W. Hall is pictured handing to Mrs. Donald Lloyd, was a special prize when Harris' staged its first formal showing of fashions since opening its store in Riverside Plaza. Completing the foursome in the picture are Marge Exter, one of the models for the benefit event, and Gwen Davison (right), Harris' style coordinator, who served as the commentator for the show. "Spring Serenade of Fashion" was chosen as the theme and featured pre-Easter apparel for the mature woman as well as the younger woman. Since 1936, when the late Ira Landis was president, the Riverside Woman's Club has been staging one event each year to raise money for various community welfare agencies. Since the Harris Company was known for its community involvement, it made sense that the event would be held at the new Riverside store.

Island Treatment in Harris', Riverside, California, March 1959. This photograph shows the basic rack fixtures used extensively throughout the store, providing flexibility and changeability for various types of merchandise.

Optometrists Shop in Harris' Riverside, March 1959. This small shop maintained the modern feeling of the selling floor and offered visual displays that emphasized self selection, both in the free-hanging shadow box and the panel on the back wall.

BETTER JEWELRY IN HARRIS' RIVERSIDE, MARCH 1959. This modern shop was a luxury setting for the discreet display and sale of jewelry. It was an intimate corner devoted to quality merchandise, which was displayed in shallow countertops and illuminated cases.

CAMPUS DEB SHOP IN HARRIS' RIVERSIDE, MARCH 1959. This attractively lit and inviting shop emphasized Campus Deb fashions. Modern signing, excellent lighting, and ample merchandise, shown on open racks, encouraged self selection.

PIN-MONEY SHOP IN HARRIS' RIVERSIDE, MARCH 1959. This attractive "Budget Shop" provided ample isle space for traffic and the showing of open stock assortments, with excellent lighting and good mirroring.

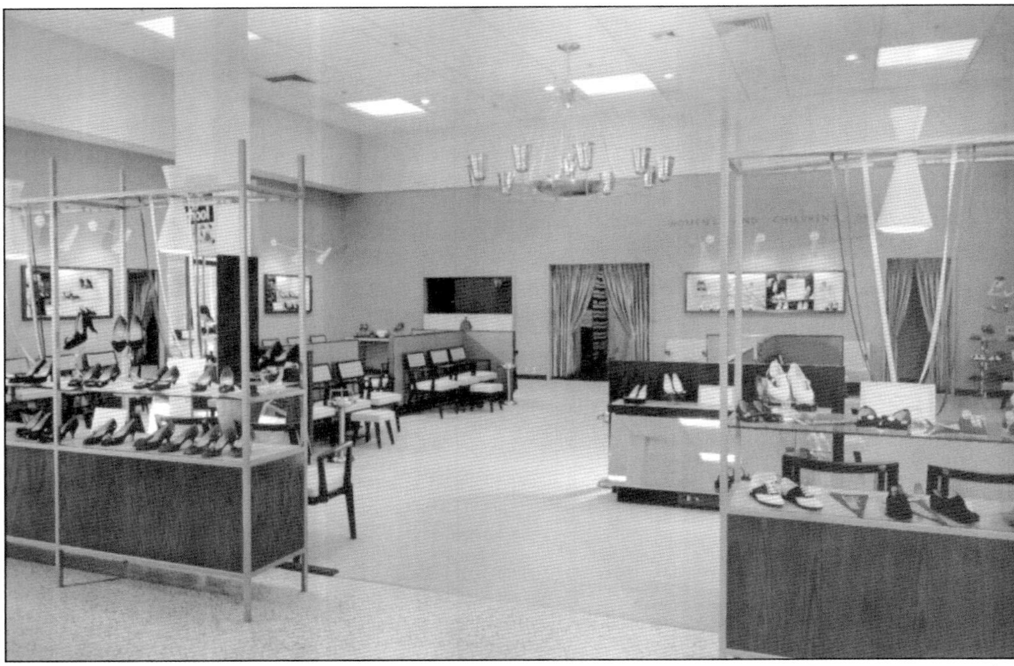

Women's and Misses' Shoes in Harris' Riverside, March 1959. This department provided a cool and pleasant setting for shoes, with a feeling of privacy, without breaking up the open airiness of the shop. A smart brass chandelier added a feeling of elegance.

Cosmetics Department in Harris' Riverside, March 1959. This shop was centrally located at the escalators in this refreshingly designed store, with its attractive visual displays and inset ceiling lights for illumination.

MEN'S VARSITY SHOP IN HARRIS' RIVERSIDE, MARCH 1959. This distinguished menswear department went all out to appeal to the college-aged trade. Merchandise was left open for self selection, with a good balance between two-tier and one-tier racks to break up the space.

MEN'S CLOTHING SHOP IN HARRIS' RIVERSIDE, MARCH 1959. A masculine air, while retaining a light atmosphere, was achieved in this shop. Vertical-grained cypress planking and brass-framed display cases break up open racks of handsome clothing.

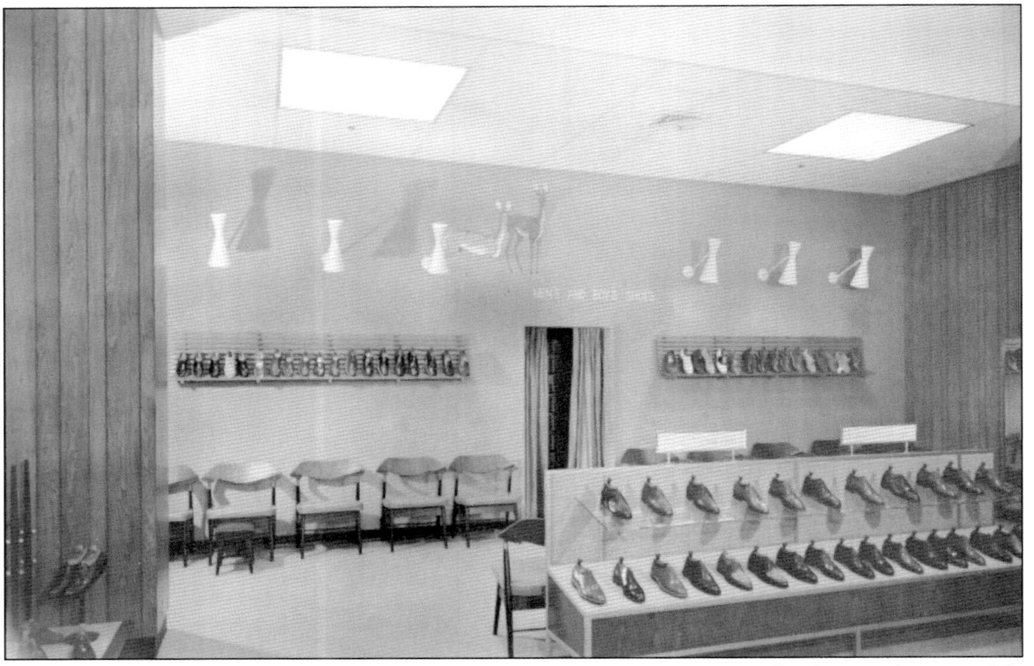

Men's and Boys' Shoes in Harris' Riverside, March 1959. Open displays made it possible to show an assortment of featured shoes, encouraged self selection, and increased the turnover of customers with hanging racks on walls and a two-level displayer.

Luggage Shop in Harris' Riverside, March 1959. The open display for luggage used a minimum amount of floor space for maximum display. The carpet-covered shelves protected the merchandise and gave it an impressive appearance.

CANDY SHOP IN HARRIS' RIVERSIDE, MARCH 1959. This candy counter featured both packaged and bulk goods displayed on well-lit shelves and the highlighted shadow box. Attention was drawn to the department by the colorful motifs and arranged for self selection.

BOOK DEPARTMENT IN HARRIS' RIVERSIDE, MARCH 1959. Browsing was encouraged, and self service was emphasized in this shop, where all bookshelves were open, and many items were displayed on tables to highlight specific titles.

NEEDLEWORK SHOP IN HARRIS' RIVERSIDE, MARCH 1959. The many colorful items in this shop attracted attention when presented in open floor displays and shelving against the surrounding wall with individual lighting.

DRAPERIES IN HARRIS' RIVERSIDE, MARCH 1959. A useful, well-lit fixture designed for this department permitted the good display of a wide assortment of drapery fabrics and patterns in a relatively small and convenient area, with a single fixture for folded goods.

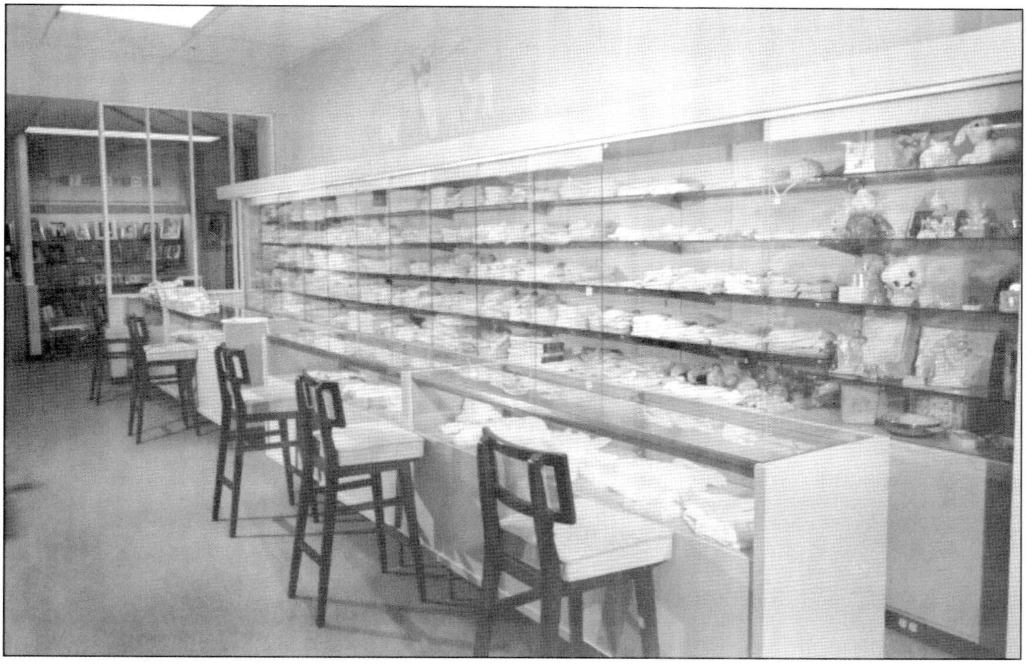

LAYETTE SHOP IN HARRIS' RIVERSIDE, MARCH 1959. Glass sliding doors protected the delicate merchandise in this shop and gave the impression of enhancing its value without detracting from the visibility. High chairs along the counter made it convenient for service.

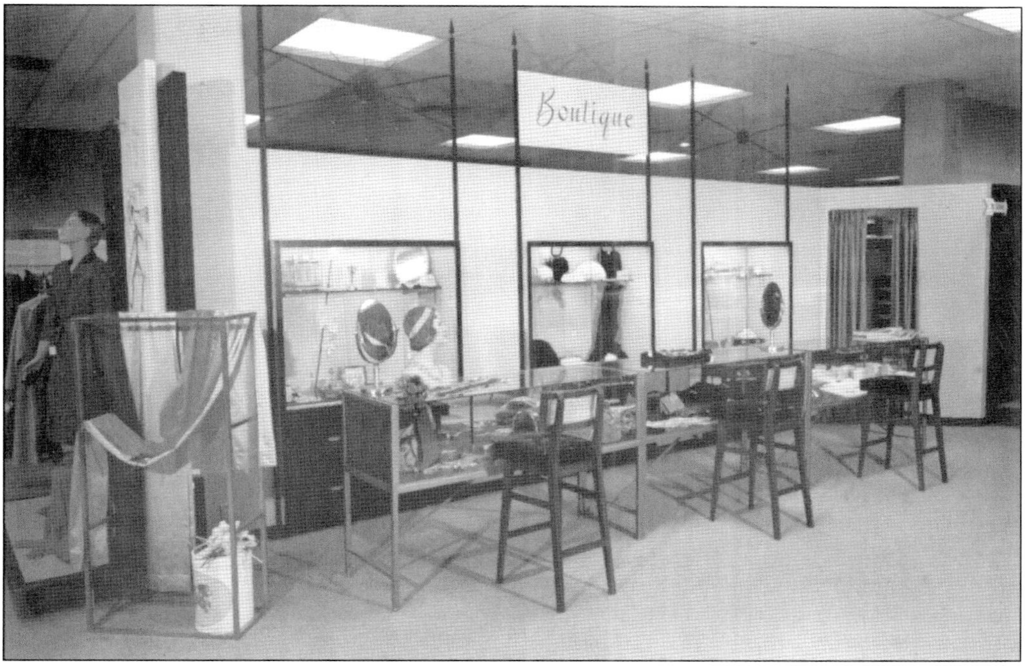

BOUTIQUE SHOP IN HARRIS' RIVERSIDE, MARCH 1959. This was a distinctive shop with a beautiful presentation of high fashion displayed in blue-toned shadow boxes framed in black with self illumination, or in the smartly designed counter unit framed in brass-tone metal.

LAMPS IN HARRIS' RIVERSIDE, MARCH 1959. This dominant, focal point, display unit promoted impulse purchases of lamps. Built to utilize a column space, it provided four-sided open visibility and space for an assortment of eye-catching items.

CHINAWARE IN HARRIS', RIVERSIDE, CALIFORNIA, MARCH 1959. The china and glassware department of the Riverside store offered a large selection of fine china in a wide variety of patterns. The plan for displaying the place settings encouraged individual selection. The department also carried beautiful silver holloware pieces and silverware.

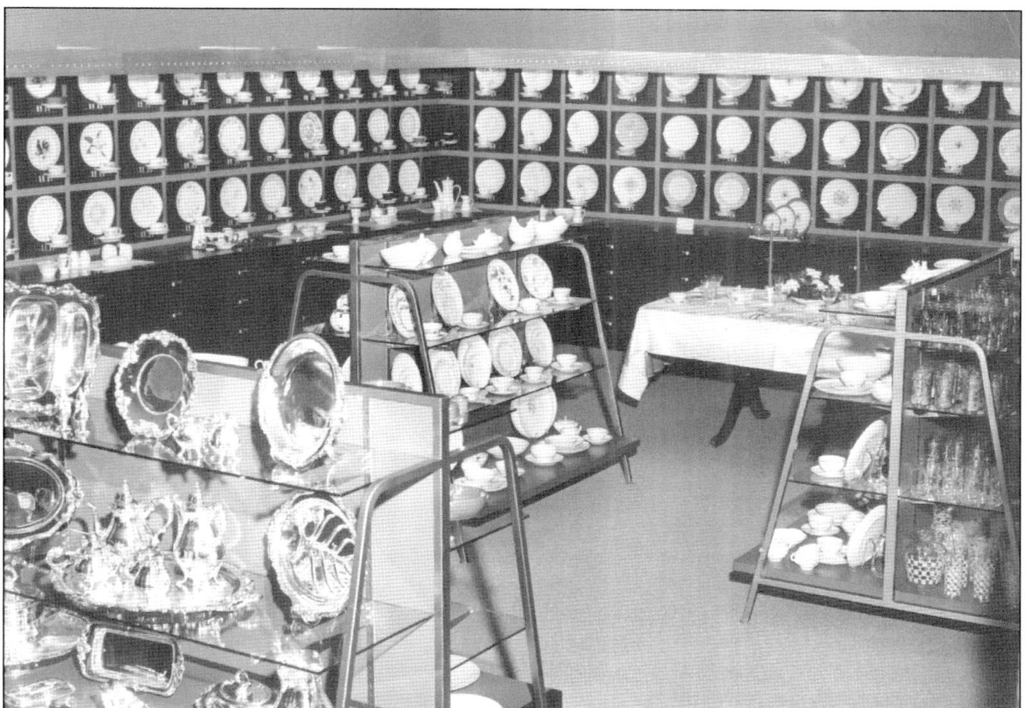

BETTER DRESSES AND BRIDAL SALON IN HARRIS' RIVERSIDE, MARCH 1959. A luxurious atmosphere was achieved in this salon-type shop, where the higher quality dresses were displayed and highlighted on islands and circular bases. The bridal salon won attention with its unique doorway, its beautiful furnishings, and its distinctive chandelier.

Ladies Lounge in Harris' Riverside, March 1959. This smartly designed setting is enhanced by brass chairs and overhead fixtures typical of the era. The lovely cove panel at the entrance created an attractive appearance.

ADVERTISEMENT FOR THE ANNUAL FASHION SHOW AT HARRIS' RIVERSIDE, AUGUST 12, 1959. Every fall in Riverside, people got the chance to view Harris' wonderful collection of clothes for the "off to college" crowd. This particular year, the store had *Mademoiselle*'s cover clothes and many other styles featured in the magazine's special college issue. The young Riverside women featured in this advertisement were Sarah Hertford, who was off to the University of California at Berkeley; Mary Jean Attride, who attended Riverside City College; Betsy Campbell, a student at Mills College; Beth Sark, who attended Stanford; Susie Barton, a student at San Jose; Betsy Veitch, who attended the University of Oregon; Sandy Swarmer, a student at the University of California at Los Angeles; Sue Anderson, who attended the University of California at Berkeley, Sue Smith, a student at the University of California at Riverside; and Phyllis Lingo, who attended the University of California at Davis.

GWEN DAVISON PRESENTING A FASHION SHOW IN HARRIS' RIVERSIDE, FALL OF 1964. This fashion show was entitled "Passport to Campus" and was one of the two major fashion shows that Davison presented at the Harris Company in Riverside each year. Every fashion show had a theme, and many hours of comprehensive work went into its preparation. Davison said, "I spend weeks selecting costumes to be shown, getting them fitted to the models, and doing the dozen and one other things that might sound small in translation but nonetheless vitally necessary to the perfectly presented style show," such as writing descriptions of each item, working with the display department to build props and backgrounds, mapping the runway order, removing tags, and making detailed lists of each article of apparel.

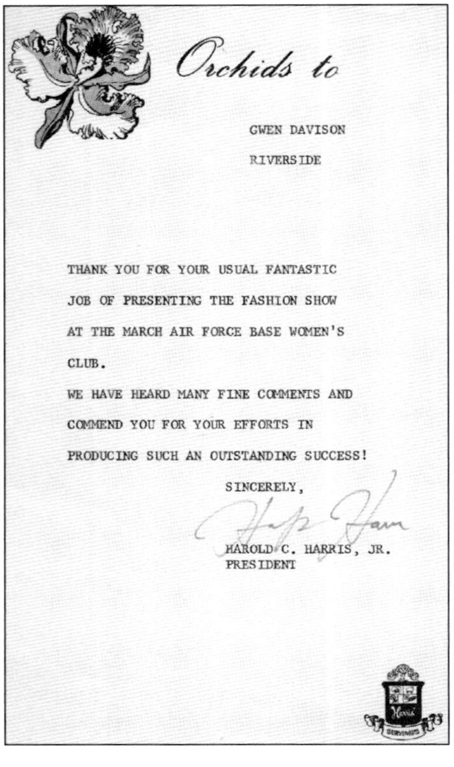

Orchids to

GWEN DAVISON

RIVERSIDE

THANK YOU FOR YOUR USUAL FANTASTIC JOB OF PRESENTING THE FASHION SHOW AT THE MARCH AIR FORCE BASE WOMEN'S CLUB.

WE HAVE HEARD MANY FINE COMMENTS AND COMMEND YOU FOR YOUR EFFORTS IN PRODUCING SUCH AN OUTSTANDING SUCCESS!

SINCERELY,

HAROLD C. HARRIS, JR.
PRESIDENT

GWEN DAVISON PRESENTING A FASHION SHOW AT HARRIS' RIVERSIDE, MAY 4, 1965. The theme of this show was "Millinery Magic," referring to hats and the business of designing, making, and selling hats and hat trim to women. A woman who purchased such a hat considered if it could be worn to luncheons and parties, and if it complemented her wardrobe, as well as her facial shape, features, and body type. In the economy of the 1960s, a woman wanted a well-rounded buy, not just a hat to be worn for one occasion. Davison narrated the show using models from Riverside to display the hats and accessories from Harris'. Davison worked for Harris' Riverside from the time it opened in 1957, and she continued to work for the store her entire career until she retired in 1980. She became a noted fashion coordinator and commentator for the beautiful fashion shows presented by the store. The letter from Harold "Hap" Harris Jr. was just one of many she received during her lifetime praising her work. (Both images courtesy of Jacqueline Davison Lee.)

WILLIAM E. ENGEL AND GWENDOLYN DAVISON OF HARRIS' RIVERSIDE, MAY 1961. Inseparably interwoven into the story of the Harris department stores of California for more than 20 years are the names William Engel and Gwendolyn Davison. The woman on the left remains unidentified. (Courtesy of Jacqueline Davison Lee.)

SHADES OF THE 1920S FASHION SHOW IN HARRIS' RIVERSIDE, MARCH 1967. Mrs. W. C. Dutton Jr. is on the left wearing a dress purchased from Worth in London in 1911, but many gowns of the 1920s resemble it. Beside her, Mrs. Clyde Pitchford is dressed in a flapper's idea of a formal. Mrs. W. LaMarr Eisenman wears a dress from the Bonnett collection, and Mrs. Donald Worley wears Hazel King Fulton's dress, purchased at the Harris Company in 1925. (Courtesy of Jacqueline Davison Lee.)

FIRST PROM DRESS, PURCHASED AT HARRIS' RIVERSIDE, CALIFORNIA, 1968. Robin Dilday, pictured here with her future husband, Richard "Lanny" Hanks, modeled this dress in a Harris Company fashion show and begged her father to buy it for her for the Poly High School Junior/Senior Prom. (Courtesy of Richard and Robin Hanks.)

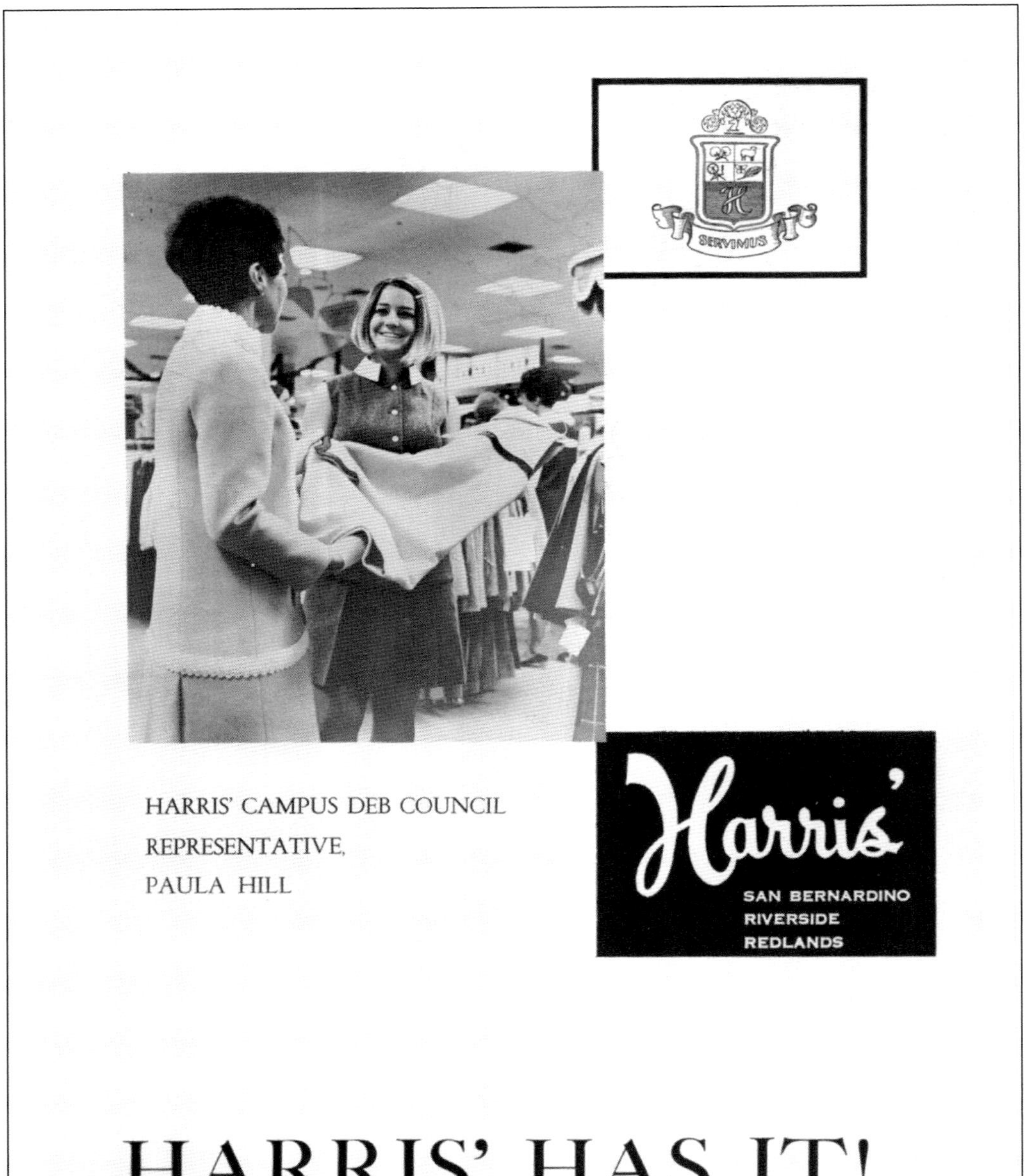

ADVERTISEMENT FOR THE HARRIS COMPANY IN THE POLY HIGH SCHOOL YEARBOOK, 1969. Every high school in Riverside had a female representative on the Campus Deb Council, and these representatives worked closely with the Harris Company to set up the fall fashion shows, as well as many other community events and fund-raisers. The Harris Company always bought advertisements in all of the high school yearbooks and supported local schools. (Courtesy of Richard and Robin Hanks.)

Five

Other Events in the Harris Company

Harris' Demonstration Sale, c. 1927. The main floor, covered in various striped and checkered tents, is reminiscent of a fair or bazaar. The long horizontal sign (left middle) reads "Albert Sheetz Mission Candies" and shows the original location of the candy department. Just to the right of the candy is a tent for "Battle Creek Sanitarium Health Foods." At the foreground (left) is a tent for "Fry's Kewpie Curlers," and chiffon hose (right) could be bought for 79¢. Whatever the item, shoppers were assured that if they bought a gift from the Harris Company, that box meant something special.

EARLY FASHION SHOW, 1919. Relocation to a new store with a second floor in 1908 enabled the introduction of fashion shows. Models used the store's aisles but later moved to the Municipal Auditorium, as shown here. From left to right are (first row) Brounette Kramer, Billie Manson, Nina Jo Rieves, unidentified, Betty McIntyre, and Lola Ford; (second row) two unidentified, Betty Robinson, three unidentified, ? Wetzel, ? Bartram, Lena ?, unidentified, and Irma Pillace; (third row) Tillie Rister, Louise Mott, and unidentified.

FIRST LOCATION OF THE HARRIS COMPANY IN INDIO, 1926. This store was managed by Jacob M. Steinart, brother-in-law of Philip Harris. Philip's second wife was Steinart's sister Leah, whom he married in 1907. In 1940, the Harris Company remodeled their building on Fargo Street. When the Indio Fashion Mall was built in 1975, Harris' became one of the anchor stores.

SILVER ANNIVERSARY, 1930. For its 25th anniversary, the Harris Company received congratulatory telegrams from San Francisco to New York. Marshall Fields in Chicago also sent flowers. The firm welcomed employees and guests in the Café Madrid, broadcasting the entire program on KFXM. Pictured here are the silver anniversary decorations on the main floor.

CELEBRITY GUEST EDNA KIRBY, 1933. During the Great Depression, the Harris Company retained Paramount Girl Edna Kirby to host the store's major attraction, "Guest Apartment" at the 1933 Orange Show. In 1928, Kirby, known as the "Girl Who Lives in Glass Houses," was mentioned in *Time* magazine for "living" in an Atlanta, Georgia, department store window. Pictured here (counter clockwise from top left) are Leslie Harris, Arthur Harris, Herman Harris, Edna Kirby, and Melville Harris.

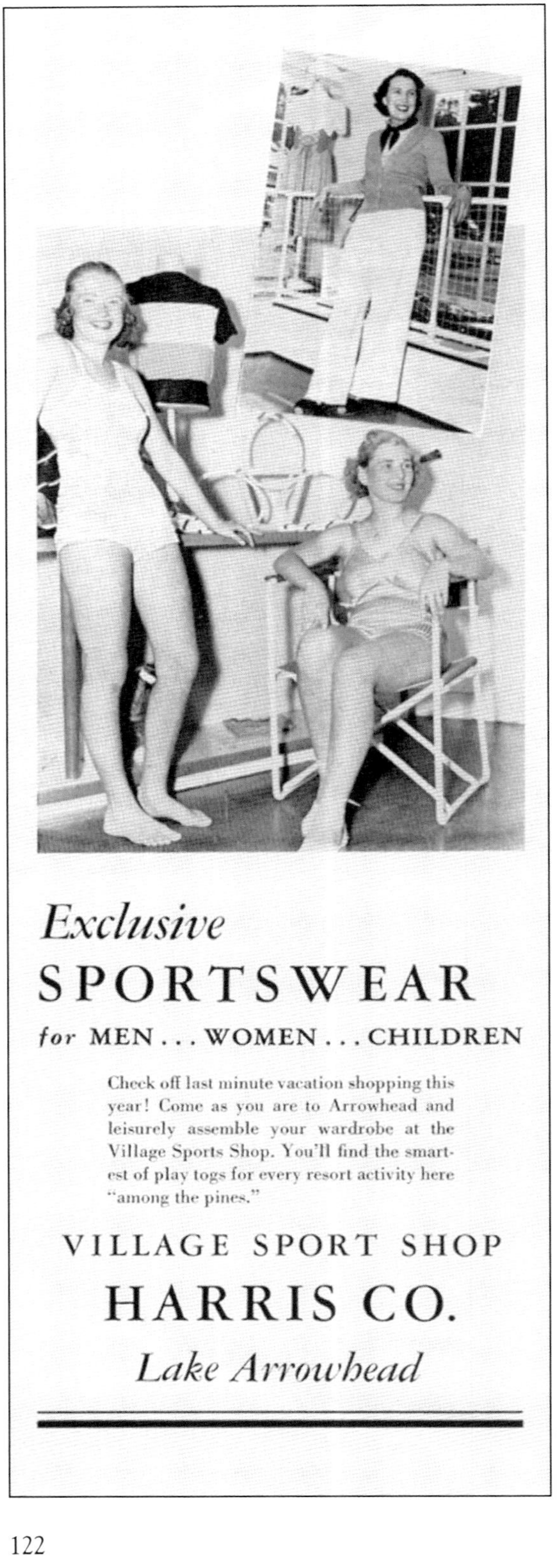

VILLAGE SPORT SHOP, LAKE ARROWHEAD, 1938. From the late 1930s to the mid-1940s, the Harris Company operated a sport shop at the Village in Lake Arrowhead. The store was opened only for the duration of the summer. Joan Harris, Leslie's eldest daughter, remembered quite a few Hollywood star sightings when she worked at the shop on her summer breaks from school. (Courtesy of John and Robin Lyles.)

ARROWHEAD SPRINGS HOTEL, C. 1945. In 1945, the Hiltons purchased the Arrowhead Springs Hotel, which overlooks the city of San Bernardino. For several years, the Harris Company operated an exclusive sportswear shop at this site. Managed by Genevieve Smith, the shop was located just off the lobby. (Courtesy of Aimmee Rodriguez.)

SAN BERNARDINO COVERED-WAGON DAYS, 1947. The program for this event noted that the Harris Company's float was the last one to represent the Spanish-Mexican era 1772–1838 in the parade. The float showed the burning of the Assistencia of San Bernardino in 1834 by local Indians, who had been stirred up by Hijar and his colonists from Mexico. Traveling on E Street, the California Hotel is visible in the background.

HARRIS COMPANY BILLBOARD. A Harris Company brochure boasted that modern freeways and highways led to Harris' and that the department store could be reached with ease from anywhere in Southern California. Pictured here is a Harris Company billboard welcoming drivers to the local mountains.

REPRESENTATIVE FOR CARE, EARLY 1950S. The Cooperative for American Relief Everywhere (CARE) was formed to meet the overwhelming needs of devastated countries in Europe after World War II. In the early 1950s, Leslie Harris was the chairman for CARE in the Inland Empire region. He is seen here on the left with his wife, Marcelle, gathering support for CARE food packages to aid families affected by the war.

Sixtieth Anniversary Advertisement for S&H Redemption Centers in Riverside, Redlands, and San Bernardino, April 24, 1965. The Harris Company started giving S&H Green Stamps with every purchase in 1909. Advertisements in the local newspapers in 1913 claimed "You could furnish your home for free. Collect all your trading stamps and fill a book. The presents you receive are so useful. Stamps are given on all goods. The premiums are exhibited at Bracewell's Grocery Store." The Harris brothers believed that the S&H Green Stamp was America's most valuable stamp because there was more gift value on the finest, top-quality, name-brand gifts. A book held 25 stamps, and a customer earned one stamp for every 10¢ spent. By 1965, more than 35 million women saved S&H Green Stamps.

Ribbon Cutting for Harris' Opening in Hemet, California, October 24, 1980. These dignitaries helped christen the Harris store at the Hemet Valley Mall. From left to right are (first row) Vic Amira; Mary Cooper; Miss San Jacinto, Kimberley Kuhlengel; Harris' general manager, Richard Cromwell III; Miss Hemet, Staci Polson; Jean Field; and Jack Hodgkins; (second row) G. Roger Brubaker; E. W. Rademacher; James W. Gill III; chamber president John Bacher; Lawrence Daugherty; and Chuck Inglett.

Harris' in Moreno Valley, 2008. This store retained the Harris' name on its building until it closed in July 2008. The decor featured multilayered geometric shapes, desert colors, and was to be one of the grandest. While the European design was completed as planned, there were no other stores built in the chain after the one in Moreno Valley. (Courtesy of Richard and Robin Hanks.)

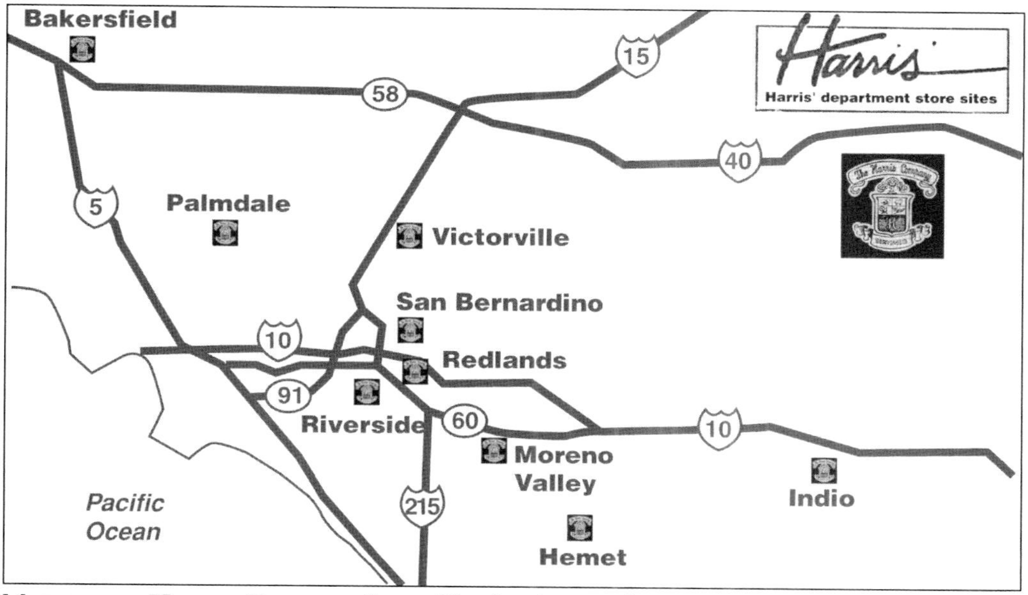

Map of the Harris Company Sites. The family-owned Harris Company grew to a chain of nine stores. Pictured here is a map of the Harris Company locations: San Bernardino (1905), Redlands (1908), Indio (1926), Riverside (1957), Hemet (1980), Victorville (1986), Bakersfield (April 1990), Palmdale (September 1990), and Moreno Valley (1993). (Courtesy of Richard and Robin Hanks.)

Removal of Harris' Sign, 2000. One year and two months after the Harris Company flagship store closed, the red, neon-lit signs were taken down. The original Harris signs were installed in 1966 then replaced with modern lettering in the 1980s. Though the signs are now gone, the structure will always remain the Harris' building to many.